Food + Architecture

Guest-edited by Karen A Franck

WILEY-ACADEMY

Architectural Design
Vol 72 No 6 Nov/Dec 2002

Editorial Offices
International House
Ealing Broadway Centre
London W5 5DB
T: +44 (0)20 8326 3800
F: +44 (0)20 8326 3801
E: architecturaldesign@wiley.co.uk

Editor
Helen Castle
Executive Editor
Maggie Toy
Production
Mariangela Palazzi-Williams
Art Director
Christian Küsters ↪ CHK Design
Designer
Scott Bradley ↪ CHK Design
Picture Editor
Famida Rasheed

Advertisement Sales
01243 843272

ISBN 0-47084570-8
Profile No 160

Abbreviated positions
t=top, b=bottom, c=centre, l=left, r=right

Cover image: Morimoto Restaurant,
Philadelphia
© Karim Rashid Inc.

AD main section
p 4 © Karim Rashid Inc.; pp 5(t&b), 6(tl&tr), 8, 12(t&c), 13(cx2), 30(t), 34, 44((l), 46(r) & 54(tl) photos: Karen Franck; pp 5(c), 9(r), 11, 12(b), 13(b), 55(tr), 58(l), 59(t), 60–1, 62(t), 63(t), 64(b) & 65–6 photos: Tony Holmes; p 6(c&b) photos: © Kathy Cacicedo; p 9(l) courtesy of Tombrock Corporation, Canaan, Connecticut; p 10 © 2002 Robert Benson; p 13(t) © Lynda Schneekloth; pp 14–5 digital renderings by ROY; p 16(l) © Laura Resen; p 16(r) © Kiwon Standen; p 18(r) © Conran Restaurants Ltd, photo: Georgia Glynn Smith; p 19 © Adam D Tihany, photo: Peter Paige; p 20 © Peter Aaron/Esto; p 21 © George Goode; p 22–4 © The Wapping Project, photo: Chris Tubbs; pp 26(t) & 49(b) © Conran & Partners; p 26(c) Moving/Mirror Image Restaurants; p 26(b) © Martin Charles; p 27(t) © St John; p 27(b) © Alan Compton Bennett; p 28 © Block Architecture, photo: Leon Chew; p 29 © Wells Mackereth Architects, photo: Paul Raeside; pp 30(b), 31 & 32(t) courtesy Hakkasan, photo: Herbert Ypma; p 32(b) courtesy Hakkasan; p 36 courtesy Hakkasan, photo: Michael Franke; p 39(l) photo: © Sandra C Rodger; p 39(r) by permission of Zhe Hu; p 40 Condé Nast Publications, Inc. / Richard Dong © 2000; p 41(t) © Ian Lambot; pp 41(b) & 90 © Foster and Partners, photo: Nigel Young; p 42 © Venturi, Scott Brown and Associates; p 43 photo: © Jamie Horwitz; pp 44(r), 45, 48 & 49(t&cx2) photo: © Gabrielle Esperdy; p 46(l) courtesy of The Rouse Company; p 47 © Greig + Stephenson; p 50 © Dennis Gilbert/VIEW; p 50(inset) © Jeff Goldberg/Esto; pp 51 & 57(l&tr) courtesy The World Monuments Fund, New York; pp 52, 53(l), 56 & 57(br) courtesy Mike's Amazing Cakes, Redmond, Washington;

pp 53(tr) & 55(br) courtesy Mike Morris; p 53(c) courtesy Rare Books Division, The New York Public Library, Astor, Lennox and Tilden Foundations; p 54(tr) © Theodore Spyropoulos (Team: Masato Ashiya, Jean Santelises, Markus Bergerheim); p 54(cl&cr) Dover Pictorial Archive Series [New York] 1983; p 55(l) © Arthur Rackham, courtesy of the artist's estate / Bridgeman Art Library; pp 58(b) & 62(c&b) © Anton Mosimann; pp 59(b), 63(b), 64(t) & 67 © Alfred Portale, photo: Gozen Koshida; pp 68–9 & 73(r) © Geoff Lung Photographic Design; p 70(t) © Russell Bell; p 70(b) courtesy Landini Associates, photo: Simon Kenny; pp 71–2 courtesy Landini Associates, photo: Ross Honeysett; p 73(l) © Simon Kenny; pp 74 & 75(l) courtesy Dale Jones-Evans, © Paul Gosney; p 76 © The Bathers' Pavilion, photo: Rodney Weidland; pp 78–9, 82, 83(r) & 84–7 © Nacasa & Partners inc.®; pp 80, 81(b), 83(l&c) & 88 © Nacasa & Partners inc.(Masayochi Yamada, Mitsuhiro Suda and Yuji Hori); p 81(tr) © Masaaki Takahashi; p 89 © Shinichi Sato; p 91 V&A Picture Library; p 92 © Adam Friedberg; pp 93 & 97 courtesy Stephan Marc Klein; p 94 © Trustees of the National Museums of Scotland; p 96 © DMCD Incorporated; pp 98–101 © Project Orange; pp 102 & 105 © Paul Smoothy; p 104 © Sarah Wigglesworth Architects.

AD+ section
pp 105+(tl&tr), 106+(b) & 107+(tr&b) courtesy Specht Harpman; pp 105+(b),106+(t) & 107+ courtesy Specht Harpman, photos: © Michael Moran; pp 108+,109+(c&cr) & 110-113+ © Mikan; p 109+(cl) courtesy Mikan, photo: ShigeruHiraga; p 114+ courtesy Mikan, photo: © Masaaki Takahashi; pp 115+,116+(tl), 117-118+ courtesy Terry Farrell & Partners, photos: Kim JaenYoun; p 116+(c&b) courtesy Terry Farrell & Partners; pp 120-122+ ©Malba/Costantini, photos: Alejandro Leveratto; p 123+ © Buro Happold; p127+ © Julian Jacobs, photos: Richard Johnson.

Subscription Offices UK
John Wiley & Sons Ltd.
Journals Administration Department
1 Oldlands Way, Bognor Regis
West Sussex, PO22 9SA
T: +44 (0)1243 843272
F: +44 (0)1243 843232
E: cs-journals@wiley.co.uk

Annual Subscription Rates 2003
Institutional Rate: UK £160
Personal Rate: UK £99
Student Rate: UK £70
Institutional Rate: US $240
Personal Rate: US $150
Student Rate: US $105
AD is published bi-monthly.
Prices are for six issues and include postage and handling charges.
Periodicals postage paid at Jamaica, NY 11431. Air freight and mailing in the USA by Publications Expediting Services Inc, 200 Meacham Avenue, Elmont, NY 11003

Single Issues UK: £22.50
Single Issues outside UK: US $45.00
Details of postage and packing charges available on request

Postmaster
Send address changes to *AD* Publications Expediting Services, 200 Meacham Avenue, Elmont, NY 11003

Printed in Italy. All prices are subject to change without notice.
[ISSN: 0003-8504]

Food+Architecture

Guest-edited by Karen A Franck

AD

Above
Opened in early 2002 in
Philadelphia, Morimoto was
designed by the industrial
designer Karim Rashid in
association with DAS Architects
as a signature space for TV
chef Masaharu Morimoto,
whose success at Nobu in
New York and on the Food
Network has been
instrumental in the US fashion
for Asian-fusion food. The
dining room is characterised
by the sculptural bas-relief
plasterwork walls and the
LED strip lighting beneath
the tables. This provides the
whole space with a variable
palette as it sets the glass
tables and partitions aglow,
and has the ability to change
between cyan, magenta,
green, orange and lilac.

There are a plethora of books on food. In terms of
architecture these are mainly confined to coffee-table books
featuring the most up-to-date restaurant designs. Surprisingly
little has been published that tackles the space of food per se,
or restaurants within the broader context of consumption.
Food + Architecture came about through a conversation
with Karen A Franck, who is currently teaching a course on
the culture of food at NJIT. Her vision of the issues involved,
as demonstrated here, are far greater than conventional
definitions. Karen has set out to make us think about the space
of food at every scale – from the arrangement of a meal on
a plate to a dining area the size of the Condé Nast Cafeteria.
Food is both an organising element for environments and
a structural ingredient, as food imitates architecture, and,
as Sarah Wigglesworth demonstrates, there are important
analogies to be drawn between cooking and construction
methods. Ultimately, though, the art of the chef and the
architect both exceed basic human requirements and are
to be enjoyed and savoured – very often conspicuously so. ∆

The Space of Food.

Inside

Outside

Free of Physical Constraints

By way of introduction to *Food + Architecture*, **Karen A Franck** chronicles the space of food, taking in everything from the agrarian field to the dinner plate. So many of the sites of food production, sale and consumption offer conviviality, pleasure and a sense of place, be it a fruit vendor on the street or a highly designed restaurant.

The space of food is all around us. Food-related activities occur in a great many places and shape much of the built environment, indoors and out. Even though the food practices of a particular period and culture influence the design of restaurants, cafés, markets, barns, fields and other spaces of food, they are also relatively free of spatial or physical constraints. In New York we encounter examples of this each day: steps or a low wall are sites of eating and drinking, pavements and car parks are popular locations for selling food, or a rooftop may become a vegetable garden. The presence of food often generates a feeling of intimacy, sometimes for just a short time, and even before we eat: a lunch truck at the side of the road, a picnic spread out on a blanket.

While the space of food is a significant part of the private domestic realm, *Food + Architecture* focuses on the public spaces of food that make up so much of the contemporary streetscape. This article explores the emergence and modification of a variety of such spaces, primarily in the northeastern US.[1]

Dining Out ●

Purchasing a prepared meal outside the home has been possible in European cities since the Middle Ages: cookshops sold hot dishes to be eaten elsewhere, and cooked the meats and other dishes brought in by townspeople who did not have the necessary oven or cooking equipment at home.[2] In 16th-century London, men could eat in alehouses, inns and taverns, and later in chophouses and coffee houses[3] (women were also permitted to eat in taverns at the time). However, in Paris, public eating choices were much more limited, primarily by the guild rules established by the Parisian cookshops that forbid the sale of individual helpings. In the colonial US, meals were provided by taverns and inns.[4]

The first establishments to be called 'restaurants' appeared in Paris in the 1760s, so named because they specialised in serving *bouillons*, or *restaurants*, to restore health and wellbeing, along with other restorative foods such as fruit, dairy products and sweets. These restaurants differed from other public eating places in that they offered a choice of foods, a menu with listed prices, flexible meal times and individual tables. The décor was also distinctive: fragile china, plentiful mirrors and landscape paintings, and candlelit tables were popular, as were private dining rooms. By the 1780s, additional, more hearty dishes were added to menus, and restaurants in Paris became not only places for meals and romantic assignations but also places of display and spectacle that could also be frequented by women.[5]

The restaurants within the pages of *Food + Architecture* descend from these original restaurants of 18th-century Paris, as well as from their predecessors within each particular city. The great number and variety of quality dining venues we now take for granted, along with their widely varying cuisines, are, however, a relatively recent phenomenon. Restaurants as such emerged in London in the mid-19th century. One of the earliest restaurants in New York, Delmonico's, opened in the 1830s and held an elaborate French meal to honour Charles Dickens in 1867.[6] But prior to the Second World War, and for some time thereafter, New York had only a handful of upscale restaurants, many of the most expensive serving French cuisine and sporting red leatherette booths or red velvet curtains.[7]

The invention of the credit card in the 1950s, the increase in world travel and the new tastes this brought with it, and the adoption of *nouvelle cuisine* and a contemporary American cuisine in the 1970s inspired by Chez Panisse in Berkeley, as well as the increase in disposable income, all contributed to the growing number of quality restaurants and the creativity in design and cuisine, particularly in the 1980s. In 1973, food writers Michael and Ariane Batterly were very pessimistic about the future of good restaurants in New York; by 1999 they were referring to the city as 'the restaurant capital of the world'.[8]

Quickly Served ●

A very different group of eating places with a much lower price range emerged across US towns and cities from the late 19th century onwards. At the time, the Industrial Revolution, combined with cheap public transport, took workers greater distances from their homes. Lunchrooms (1869), horsedrawn lunch wagons (1872), cafeterias (1885), luncheonettes (1880s), automats (1892) and diners (1924) all offered low-cost, quickly available meals cooked on site, as did the first hamburger chains of the 1920s, which were open 24 hours a day. Design ingenuity and market savvy marked the invention and modification of many of these types of eating places. Lunchrooms, mainly serving men, might provide only one-armed chairs where customers placed their trays. Catering to women and children as well as men, luncheonettes and, later, coffee shops (1920s) adopted the soda-fountain counter, which originally served ice-cream sodas, and began to offer sandwiches, soups and other items. Tall stools at tall counters, a remnant of the earlier taverns, were lowered in the 1890s to meet the needs of women and children, and were then designed in U-shapes so that customers opposite each other might converse, and in order that one employee could serve more people from a single position.[9]

The diner, a distinctively American restaurant type, evolved from a horsedrawn 'night lunch wagon' in Providence, Rhode Island, which in 1872 began its rounds after other eating places closed at 8pm. As then, the diners of today are expected to serve only homemade items and are known particularly for their pies. Eventually designed to stay put after delivery, and serving breakfast, lunch and dinner, what had become 'lunch cars' became diners in the 1920s. Built almost invariably in factories and towed to sites by truck, all had the signature long marble counter running the length of the car. By 1924, an O'Mahoney diner came with all equipment and supplies included. Like lunch cars, diners attracted only men until the mid-1920s when manufacturers began to offer tables or booths in addition to counters.

In the 1930s, diners adopted the streamlined look of locomotives, featuring stainless-steel and porcelain enamel exteriors. In the 1940s and 1950s they grew in size to accommodate the increase in families eating out. However, in the 1960s tastes changed, with some

Above
Restaurants, Rockefeller
Center Plaza, New York.
The plaza (built in 1933) was
always intended to be used
for dining in summer and
skating in the winter.

Right
Twenty-first-century lunch,
Bryant Park, New York.
The park has a new wireless
Internet connection.

localities even forbidding stainless-steel buildings and the use of the word 'diner'. Kullman Dining Car Company, established in 1927, became Kullman Industries and began to build brick-clad 'colonial diners'.[10] Now, however, there is great affection for traditional diners: some are listed on the National Register of Historic Places, and many have been restored or moved to new locations (one to Barcelona). In addition, several chain restaurants have adopted the diner image, and Kullman recently installed two diners in Germany (these were built in New Jersey and assembled on site).

The biggest US contribution to a global foodscape, however, has been fast-food chains. The first hamburger chains, White Castle (1920) and then, with conscious imitation, White Tower (1926) chose a repetitive and easily identifiable design of very small porcelain enamel buildings. These could be immediately associated with the food they served – hamburgers made to order. White Castle was the first large restaurant company to adopt a uniform building image (followed quickly by White Tower); it advertised its commitment to consistency in design and food, in contrast to the unpredictability of lunchrooms and diners.[11]

The first chain restaurants were in cities, but with the increase in driving, roadside eateries, or drive-ins, emerged where carhops (waiting staff) delivered food to your car (there was no interior space for eating). The postwar period saw the emergence of roadside ice-cream stands of standardised design (for example Dairy Queen and Carvel), and then in 1949 the first McDonald's, an octagonal-shaped drive-in with a rigidly standardised menu and the self-service format once common to cafeterias and automats. The resultant decrease in labour costs, speed of service and low prices gained nationwide attention and, eventually, made McDonald's and

other self-service chains serving standardised pre-cooked food an international form of eating out. Today, a roadside strip in the US is likely to be an endless parade of McDonald's, Burger King, Pizza Hut, Kentucky Fried Chicken and Taco Bell, each with its distinctive yet standardised and forgettable building, each with its asphalt forecourt.

Eating Outdoors

People take great pleasure in eating outside, and the restaurant garden, lunch truck, hot-dog stand and ice-cream truck all invite customers to do so, as do sidewalk cafés, picnic tables and public barbecue grills. Eating outdoors in a garden or at a picnic has long been acceptable. In the US, before the advent of public parks, people enjoyed picnics in cemeteries. Today, on holiday weekends, New York City parks designed by Frederick Law Olmsted are filled with families and friends barbecuing, eating and playing games. New Yorkers bring elaborate picnics to Central Park for summer concerts of opera and classical music, and each summer weekend street fairs offer a variety of ethnic foods.

For some reason, women have been freer to eat outdoors than in indoor establishments. In 18th-century London, respectable women could eat in the many tea and pleasure gardens but not in coffee houses, taverns or chophouses.[12] Even in the 1940s in Paris, in an effort to control prostitution, Simone de Beauvoir was asked, since she was alone, to sit at an outdoor table at the Dome.[13] At the same time, eating on the street, by men *or* women, without the benefit of a café, has carried some stigma as being crude and uncivilised.[14] However, this is now changing as the distinctions between appropriate places and times to eat become ever more fluid (see Jamie Horwitz's article, 'Working Lunch'). In the 1990s, the mayor of New York tried to remove the numerous lunch trucks from the pavements of midtown Manhattan, but met with such vehement public resistance that he backed down.

The opportunity to eat outdoors comfortably is now prized as an important source of urban vitality. William H

Above right
White Tower, New York (1933). White Towers were open 24 hours a day and food was cooked to order. From Paul Hirshorn and Steven Izenour, *White Towers*, MIT Press (Cambridge, Mass), 1979.

Far right
A 19th-century café scene. From *Food and Drink*, Dover Publications (Mineola, NY), 1983.

Above
Exterior of Portland Public Market, Portland, Maine (Hugh A Boyd Architects, 1998). Newly built, with a skybridge to the garage, the market is intended to help revitalise the downtown, provide opportunities for small businesses and strengthen the region's agriculture. Boyd used materials made in Maine, and employed local tradespeople.

Right
The interior of Portland Public Market houses 28 permanent vendors and eight day-stalls. Architect Hugh Boyd installed a decorative grid that combines track lighting with a display system for hanging fresh food.

Whyte cited this as key to successful urban public spaces and recommended that it be incorporated into public open spaces.[15] As a result, builders in Manhattan are granted the right to build extra floors if they provide a public space with specific amenities, including sites for food vendors. Similarly, zoning in many US towns and cities has been amended to allow cafés and restaurants to place tables and chairs on the pavement outside their establishments. Urban designer Jan Gehl's recommendation for incentives for outdoor cafés in Copenhagen initially met with scepticism as these were an Italian custom, not Scandinavian. The cafés are so successful that in the autumn they provide blankets for chilly customers.

Buying and Growing

We have moved from pushcarts on the street, market stalls and small grocery shops to large supermarkets where choice products that lack any true differences is overwhelming. As Sarah Wigglesworth points out in 'Cuisine and Architecture', the food is from both everywhere and nowhere in particular. And so is the

supermarket building – nothing about it hints at where it might be. In addition, anything could be inside; only signs in the window tell us there is food to be bought. Internally, the smell and look of the food is suppressed by air conditioning, lighting and packaging. The bland space of the supermarket extends well beyond the building to meet the requirements for bulk transport and car parking. The supermarket joins fast-food chains in its standardisation of food and its appearance.[16]

Fortunately, we are rediscovering alternatives to the supermarket, as Gabrielle Esperdy demonstrates in 'Edible Urbanism'. The preservation and renovation of market buildings, such as Spitalfields in London or Reading Terminal in Philadelphia, and the insertion of food markets into existing buildings of architectural merit, not only bring quality produce and choice food products to urban residents, but also contribute significantly to the appearance of the city, as the grand produce- and meat-markets once did, and as supermarkets so sorely do not. Fresh food markets benefit farmers, residents and restaurants, and increase

Fresh food markets benefit farmers, residents and restaurants, and increase the viability and vitality of urban life.

Top
Potato field, Martin Sidor
Farms, Mattituck, New York.
The same family has grown
potatoes here for three
generations, since 1910.
Much of the crop is now sold
to Puerto Rico. In the distance
is a vineyard. The first
commercial Long Island
vineyard was planted in 1973.
Now there are 4000 acres of
vineyards; some are owned
by large investors and the
price of farmland has
increased dramatically.

Bottom
Potato barn, Peconic, New
York. Placement in the earth
keeps the interior cool in
summer and warm in winter.

Notes
1. For other discussions of food
and space, see David Bell and
Gill Valentine, *Consuming
Geographies*, Routledge
(London), 1997, and Jamie
Horwitz and Paulette Singley
(eds), *Eating Architecture*, MIT
Press (Cambridge, Mass), 2003.
2. Stephen Mennell, *All
Manners of Food*, University of
Illinois Press (Urbana), 1996.
3. Edwina Ehrman, Hazel
Forsyth, Lucy Peltz and Cathy
Ross, *London Eats Out*, Philip
Wilson (London), 1999.
4. Richard Pillsbury, *From
Boarding House to Bistro*,
Unwin Hyman (Boston), 1990.
5. Rebecca L Spang, *The
Invention of the Restaurant*,
Harvard University Press
(Cambridge, Mass), 2000.
6. Michael and Ariane Batterly,
On the Town in New York,
Routledge (New York), 1999.
7. Patrick Kuh, *The Last Days
of Haute Cuisine*, Penguin
(New York), 2001.

the viability and vitality of urban life. The Rudy Bruner Award for Urban Excellence has recognised this role of markets in premiating Pike Place Market in Seattle (1987), the Greenmarket programme in New York (1991) and the Portland Public Market in Maine (1999).[17]

Chronologically speaking, the first space of food is the farm. Here too we have seen increases in size, homogenisation and standardisation. Traditionally the buildings for storing the harvest, animals and machinery made up the vernacular architecture of a particular region, employing local materials and responding to local needs and constraints. Not only do these

contribute to the beauty of the landscape, they also allow us to recognise a place: the gambrel-roofed barns of Pennsylvania, the half-buried potato barns of Long Island or the grain elevators of Buffalo. With the development of agribusiness and corporate farming, farm buildings have become standardised and prefabricated, with little recognisable association to food (anything could be inside them) and with no connection to a particular location. In the Midwest, for example, even the fibreglass silos which came to symbolise the landscape are being replaced by horizontal structures only six or seven feet high.[18]

In the US, what is harvested comes from extremely large, homogeneous fields as well, owned by large and distant corporations. To serve the large-scale operations of fast-food chains and supermarkets, and for economies of scale and efficiency, farms have become more like factories, or the farmland may have gone completely, replaced by subdivisions, office parks and shopping centres. Fortunately, farmers' markets in cities throughout the country are saving many local farms and

thereby helping to preserve some of the farming landscape. Following the tenets established by *nouvelle cuisine*, restaurants are buying fresh, local produce, and therefore becoming an important market for farms in the region.

Without the benefit of any greenbelt programme, rural counties are attempting to adopt zoning and planning restrictions, and to provide financial incentives to farmers to limit development and preserve agricultural uses. In some areas, such as eastern Long Island, new forms of agriculture are replacing previous ones: vineyards, nurseries and tree farms, or specialised organic farms that sell directly to restaurants, take the place of potato and corn fields, dairy or vegetable farms. Some long-time farmers may add prepared food – roasted corn or strawberry shortcake – to the produce at their roadside stands, and incorporate family entertainment – corn mazes, hay rides and pick-your-own strawberries or pumpkins. Vineyards host other forms of entertainment: wine tastings, tours, free concerts, art exhibitions and cooking demonstrations.

A Sense of Community and Continuity

Being able to visit a public place of refreshment regularly, to linger and socialise, gives people an alternative to home and work – a 'third place'.[19] Several single elderly men gather each day in the diner in Cutchogue, New York. The waitress reports that one comes for both lunch and dinner every day. The luncheonette counter at the Coronet in Greenport fulfils a similar role. In Hong Kong, Taipei and Seoul, none other than McDonald's offers a third place where women and children spend entire afternoons sitting, chatting, doing homework.[20] Working alone, writers and artists may find the third place particularly important. Isaac Bashevis Singer and other struggling writers recently arrived in New York from eastern Europe often met at cafeterias and automats. Jackson Pollock, Willem de Kooning and other abstract Expressionist painters gravitated to the Cedar Tavern, and since 1963 Elaine's has attracted writers and editors.

Third places generate a sense of community and offer an opportunity for political discourse, as in the early London coffee houses described by Samantha Hardingham in 'Sit Facing In'. By banning any form of commercial establishment, including cafés, bars and restaurants, from residential areas, US suburbs have essentially eliminated the third place and the chance for the sense of community and belonging they generate.

Spaces of food bring economic and social viability to communities, regardless of the quality of the architecture or the food. Many poor neighbourhoods throughout the US suffer from a lack of spaces of food. One significant sign of revitalisation is the arrival of a Pathmark supermarket or a Kentucky Fried Chicken, often created as a freestanding building surrounded by parking, even in

Top
Restaurant-dining in the former waiting room, Union Station, Washington DC (Daniel Burnham, 1907). The luxurious spaces of the original station were converted to restaurants and shops in 1988; waiting now takes place in an extension, in much more modest spaces as consumption replaces service.

Middle
Prospect Heights Community Farm, Brooklyn. Local residents grow flowers, vegetables, fruit and herbs in what was an empty site, with the guidance of the Green Thumb organisation. Residents have developed similar gardens throughout New York; however, the city government is now reclaiming many of the sites to build housing.

Bottom
The Big Duck, Flanders, New York (1931). Once a farm stand selling Long Island ducks and immortalised in Robert Venturi and Denise Scott Brown's distinction between 'duck buildings' and 'decorated sheds' (*Learning from Las Vegas*, 1972). They used the photograph from Peter Blake's *God's Own Junkyard: The Planned Deterioration of America's Landscape* (1964, revised 1979). The building is now listed on the National Register of Historic Places.

Opposite
Top
Standard Elevator, A E Baxter, 1928 (additions 1942). One of five Buffalo grain elevators still used to unload grain from freighters, store it and transfer it to trains. The massive concrete structures inspired Le Corbusier, Walter Gropius and other European architects (see Reyner Banham, *A Concrete Atlantis*, MIT, 1986). The remaining elevators have been nominated for listing on the National Register of Historic Places.

Middle top
Martha Clara Vineyard, Riverhead, New York.

Middle bottom
Mooi café, London. Co-owner Anthony Meyer took great care in selecting glassware, cutlery and dishes, choosing white dishes for the summer and red/brown for the winter.

Bottom
Space of food and pleasure on a smaller scale. *Paquet* of pineapple and crème fraîche sorbet, Fleur de Sel, New York. Pastry chef Yvan Lemoine takes great care in inventing and presenting desserts.

cities where buildings abut the pavement (although in Harlem, Pathmark was required to place parking on the roof). The arrival of a gourmet food store or café signals a different kind of revitalisation and a different anticipated population.[21] Both are more likely to be installed in existing structures, maintaining the sense of place derived from the architecture while reflecting a change in use, often from production or service to consumption. As shown in this issue, restaurateurs will take on a bathers' pavilion in Sydney, a taxi garage in New York and a meat market in London.

Over and over again, spaces of food contribute to the specificity and recognisability of a place when they attend to what is local. Historic markets and newly constructed buildings offer outlets for selling local produce and contribute to a sense of community. One of the goals of the Portland Public Market is to 'create a place where people from Portland's various economic groups mix freely and where the region's food and agriculture traditions are celebrated'. Community gardens in New York City convert abandoned sites to lush greenery, allowing people to grow their own fruit and vegetables and providing places to meet one's neighbours. Maintaining an agricultural landscape helps preserve the identity and historic continuity of a region, even when this depends upon 'agritainment' and 'agritourism'.

Spaces of food also become a kind of prosaic historic monument, for example the Big Duck on Long Island, the Buffalo grain elevators and traditional diners now listed as historic sites. Many of the places illustrated in this article may seem quaint or romantic in the context of our contemporary world of standardised food and standardised spaces of food consumption. But it is these places that help create continuity and community, and it is these places that give us pleasure.[22]

The Pleasures of Food ●━━━━━━
Certainly eating is pleasurable. However, what is more remarkable are the various pleasures that accrue around the act of eating – the pleasures of growing food or at least picking it, and the visual pleasure of displays of produce for sale or still growing.

The presence of food and the anticipation of eating seem to create an atmosphere of comfort and informality, a softening of the situation, encouraging participants to feel more relaxed and to enjoy themselves, even if they are alone. Perhaps this is one reason why we now see food for sale virtually everywhere – in museums (as described by Stephan Klein in 'Museum (Quality) Dining'), book shops, galleries, boutiques and even hair salons. And perhaps it is for this reason, as well as the sensory stimulation of food, that public places of refreshment serve as places of inspiration. Writing guru Natalie Goldberg recommends writing in cafés and restaurants: the 'atmosphere keeps that sensory part of you busy and happy so that the deeper and quieter part of you that

8. Batterly, op cit.

9. Philip Langdon, *Orange Roofs, Golden Arches*, Alfred Knopf (New York), 1986.

10. Richard J S Gutman, *American Diner*, Johns Hopkins University Press (Baltimore), 1993.

11. Langdon, op cit; John A Jakle and Keith A Sculle, *Fast Food*, Johns Hopkins Press (Baltimore), 1999; Paul Hirshorn and Steven Izenour, *White Towers*, MIT Press (Cambridge, Mass), 1979.

12. Ehrman et al, op cit.

13. Simone de Beauvoir, *Letters to Sartre*, trans and ed Quintin Hoare, Arcade (New York), 1992.

14. Gill Valentine, 'Food and the production of the civilised street', in Nicholas R Fyfe (ed) *Images of the Street*, Routledge (London), 1998.

15. William H Whyte, *The Social Life of Small Urban Spaces*, Conservation Fund (Washington DC),1980; William H Whyte, *City: Rediscovering the Center*, Doubleday (New York), 1989.

16. Murray Silverstein and Max Jacobson, 'Restructuring the hidden program', in Wolfgang Preiser (ed) *Programming the Built Environment*, Van Nostrand Reinhold (New York), 1985.

17. See Philip Langdon, *Urban Excellence*, Van Nostrand Reinhold (New York), 1990, and Jay Farbstein and Richard Wener, *Connections*, Brunner Foundation (New York), 1992.

18. Hemalata Dandekar, 'Farm type in the American Midwest', in Karen A Franck and Lynda H Schneekloth (eds) *Ordering Space*, Van Nostrand Reinhold (New York), 1994.

19. Ray Oldenburg, *The Great Good Place*, Paragon House (New York), 1989.

20. James L Watson (ed) *Golden Arches East*, Stanford University Press (Stanford), 1997.

21. See Sharon Zukin, 'Gentrification, cuisine and the critical infrastructure', in *Landscapes of Power*, University of California (Berkeley), 1991.

22. The foods themselves give us a sense of continuity and pleasure as well. The international movement Slow Food is dedicated to protecting 'the right to taste' against the threats of industrial standardisation of food. Activities include the identification and support of products, dishes and animals that are in danger of extinction, and the promotion of sensory education and food culture.

23. Natalie Goldberg, *Writing Down the Bones*, Shambhala (Boston), 1986, p 92.

24. Kuh, op cit.

> Spaces of food contribute to the specificity and recognisability of a place when they attend to what is local.

creates and concentrates is free to do so'.[23] Walk into a Starbucks in New York today and note the number of patrons ensconced with their laptops.

Since its invention in 18th-century Paris, the restaurant has been envisioned as a place of display and sensuous luxury. Expensive New York restaurants in the 1940s took this, and the coupling of restaurant to consumption, to an extreme when they displayed diamonds from the best jewellers to encourage diners to visit their shops.[24] Today there is a much wider variety of restaurant venues serving a more varied public, yet the intent to give the diner visual as well as gastronomic pleasure remains paramount. Sheridan Rogers shows that 'On the Waterfront' in Sydney, this is achieved with wide expanses of glass and generous views of the harbour, while in Tokyo, as Masaaki Takahashi demonstrates, dining and drinking have an inward focus in dim, mysterious retreats.

However, making a place of eating truly special does not have to be limited to expensive restaurants. As described by Helen Castle, restaurateur Alan Yau made that very clear at Wagamama in London. Architect James Soane even brings quality design to takeaway outlets on the high street (see 'Menu-Driven Design' by Helen Castle). In addition we are beginning to see salad bars and quick-service restaurants in New York that are aesthetically enjoyable places to linger.

Another culinary tradition from France is the aesthetic pleasure of food artfully created or imaginatively arranged on the plate (see my article, 'Design on the Plate', and Mark Morris's 'Architecture Yum!'). At this scale of the space of food there is also the kinaesthetic pleasure of a sufficiently heavy fork or glass, a well-designed cup and a gracious plate. The advent of the first restaurants brought these pleasures, previously available only in private homes and palaces and reserved for members of the court, the aristocracy and their guests, to the public, so that anyone who could afford to could enjoy the visual as well as the gustatory pleasures of elaborate dining. Festive meals have long involved elements of display and entertainment; in our age of consumption and spectacle we have brought these pleasures to a much wider public and incorporated them into shopping for food as well as eating it. Δ

Eating Out
in New York:

All This World's a Stage

In no city in the world do restaurants play the role in daily life that they do in New York. The line between the celluloid and real life almost disappears when diners become actors, and actors pose as diners. **Jayne Merkel** describes how New York restaurants are a two-way film mirror – reflecting life and then Hollywood back to us. This, she explains, has led to a heightened sense of design fed by the desire of New Yorkers to see and be seen, and to ultimately be part of the action.

Audrey Hepburn may have had *Breakfast at Tiffany's*, but actors in the New York films of today go to restaurants, like the locals they portray. In Manhattan, even intimate events like weddings and birthday parties take place in public restaurants with strangers looking on; privacy disappeared with the telephone booth.

Meg Ryan proves this in *When Harry Met Sally* by faking an orgasm for Billy Crystal, with full sound effects, in the middle of a busy deli. And, without skipping a beat, Olympia Dukakis, seated at the next table, tells her waitress: 'I'll have what she's having'.

The scene works partly because the deadpan action is set in a real place (the 201 Delicatessen in Tribeca, which is still in business – quietly). But the directors of *It Could Happen to You* couldn't find a diner ordinary looking enough where Nicholas Cage could tip waitress Bridget Fonda with a lottery ticket that turned out to be a winner. So they built one on a vacant site – on anything-but-ordinary West Broadway.

Baudrillard might have loved it, but that particular brand of fakery is out of tune with this town. Banality is the one thing New Yorkers deplore – that's why chain restaurants play such a minor role.

In New York, drama rules. Something akin to set design creates the right backdrop for real life. All this world's a stage. While the Hollywood crew were working their banal magic on West Broadway, a few blocks northeast on Spring Street restaurateur Keith McNally was creating Balthazar, a SoHo brasserie that recalls turn-of-the-century Paris so convincingly that patrons in modern dress look a little out of place there. Fortunately (or purposely?), the frosted glazing on the Art Nouveau patterned windows keeps the people just slightly out of view, and that way you have to come in to see who's there.

New Yorkers love this grand sham – so much that it spawned a dozen similar period pieces, each unique, owned by different people, and seemingly

aged to perfection. The rage Balthazar became when it opened in 1997 is immortalised in 'Sex in the City' when Carrie and her friends endure rebuffs from the haughty *maître dame* who stands guard there – until Samantha encounters her in the ladies room in desperate need of a tampon. After that, the girls go right to the front of the line. Such is the fragility of the New York power scene and the way restaurants define it.

Balthazar and its progeny – L'Express in Flatiron, Pastis and Markt in the meat-packing district, Lucien and Resto Léon in the East Village, Patois and Bar Tabac on Smith Street in Brooklyn – were not the city's first bistros. La Goulue on Madison Avenue, Les Halles in Murray Hill, Felix in SoHo and the Odeon (the Tribeca standby brought to fame in *Bright Lights Big City*) all predate them. What distinguishes the recent arrivals is a certain over-the-top verisimilitude, an attempt to re-create the experience of being in France (or Belgium) – by actually importing panelling, bars, furniture or decorative details from old European cafés – or copying them so convincingly that the line between fantasy and reality is blurred.

In 1999, restaurant tsar Daniel Bouley took this trend to its epitome at Danube, an exuberant take on a turn-of-the-19th-century Viennese café in a wedged-shaped building in Tribeca, complete with larger-than-life-size fake Gustav Klimt murals. The art may be tongue in cheek but the chef makes gastronomic art out of stolid Viennese fare. 'Theatrical' doesn't begin to describe this place – it's Cecil B De Mille in 3-D.

Curiously, the re-creations appeared in the 1990s when the retro style of the previous decade was giving way to minimalism in clothing, boutiques and galleries. The hard-edged industrial chic that triumphed in residential lofts and dot.com offices barely made headway in restaurants. Cena on East 22nd Street, a pristine study in green glass and stainless steel which won awards for its equally minimalist food, closed within a year or two. Space was palpable in this high-ceilinged, sparsely furnished space, and the detailing was deft. The place was the apotheosis of cool, but it must have intimidated customers, for even a rash of rave reviews couldn't keep it alive. It didn't look like a 'scene'. (Tsao & McKown's equally icy and elegant Metrazur did survive, but this may be because it is tucked into a vault in Grand Central Station, overlooking the frenzy below.)

New Yorkers want to be part of the action – why else would they eat bland boiled hot dogs on crowded street corners, munch on the front steps of the Metropolitan Museum or lunch on barren plazas next to bland modern office buildings? If they were just trying to save time, they would eat at their desks as do people in suburban office buildings, and they would eat the same fast food as those across the rest of the US. In New York, only artfully wrapped fare from a gourmet deli will do. Despite food snobbery and the health-food craze, the hot-dog vendors (who also sell doughy salted pretzels, bottled water and soft drinks from wheeled carts) are as much fixtures of the New York City street scene as traffic lights and yellow taxis. In recent years, competition from ethnic vendors purveying spicy shish kebabs or tacos has arrived with the latest immigrant waves – they'll probably survive and multiply as they add to the cacophony. Street life is what people come to New York for– the rush that comes from fast-walking crowds, honking taxis, flashing lights, moving signs and death-defying cyclists.

How can a restaurant designer compete with all that?

One way would be to idealise and frame the restaurant for consumption. Another would be to make it a 'scene' in its own right. This is, of course, easier said than done. However, Philip Johnson managed to do it so successfully at the Four Seasons in the Seagram Building in 1959 that it is still ranked number one in the city, by décor, in the *Zagat's* guide, which is based on a survey of diners' preferences. There was a time, in the 1970s and 1980s, when critics thought that modern design was a bore, but this pristine rectangular series of rooms with Tugendhat chairs, wall-to-wall carpeting, cool lighting and a processional sequence that allows patrons to see and be seen without appearing to want to, has made the Four Seasons the favourite of the power elite for all these years. It has never gone out of style.

> There was a time, in the 1970s and 1980s, when critics thought that modern design was a bore.

Neither has restaurateur Danny Meyer's Union Square Cafe, which opened in 1985, was designed by Bogdanow Partners Architects and comes in first overall (for food, décor, service and value) in the *Zagat* survey year after year. Meyer went on to create half a dozen of the city's most popular restaurants nearby. From a design standpoint, the main innovation was putting the dining room in the window where passers-by can see his customers enjoying themselves comfortably in a pleasant but unspectacular yellow-walled room, each table spotlighted by halogen bulbs that turn patrons into unselfconscious actors. Every dish is superbly prepared, every waiter and waitress trained to make guests feel at ease. Meyer, like Mies, seems to believe: 'I don't want to be interesting. I want to be good'.

Before he opened his next restaurant, Gramercy Tavern, nine years later, Meyer and his architects Peter and Paul Bentel toured European country restaurants and wineries to see what worked best. As a result, the cavernous space in a loft building on East 20th Street has a slightly tavernous feel – half-timber and halogen. It also has murals of food by artist Robert Kushner on the upper walls of the bar, which is more commodious than that at the Union Square Cafe and serves casual meals. This is the room where big windows, set between copper Corinthian columns, entice people walking by. As a kind of enhanced loft, Gramercy Tavern resembles the Gotham Bar and Grill, a slightly more

above 14th Street in 1811. Though several plots are combined in tall buildings, street-level retail space is usually divided into the shoe-box shape. Most restaurants have a bar at the front along one wall by the window. The rest cries out for decoration.

In the city's oldest surviving restaurants that decoration recalled an English pub – rough stucco walls framed by heavy dark-wood timbers, bare floors and plain wood tables or booths. After all, the Bridge Cafe (1794) on Water Street in the financial district, Pete's Tavern (1864) in Gramercy Park, McSorley's Ale House in Greenwich Village (1860s) were all primarily saloons (McSorley's didn't admit women until as late as the 1970s).

Taverns were around from the first settlements, but it wasn't until 1831 that the first real restaurant in New York – and in America – opened when the Delmonico brothers, John and Peter, from Ticino, Switzerland, turned their confectionery on William Street into a proper French restaurant with formal dinners of a kind then known only in Paris (and even there in a public restaurant for little more than fifty years). After the great fire of 1835, the brothers and their nephews, who had joined them in the business, built a grandiose three-storey structure on the acute angle of the corner of William and Beaver streets, with Pompeian columns at the entrance.

dramatic New American classic, designed by architect James Biber of Pentagram, which opened on East 12th Street the year before the Union Square Cafe. Here, fluffy curtained chandeliers punctuate the big, open, two-level space which, like the Four Seasons, encourages promenade and manages to achieve a certain elegance without appearing to try.

Some of the most romantic restaurants in New York compete with the street scene by putting the skyline on stage. The Art Deco Rainbow Room at the top of 30 Rockefeller Center, which was renovated by Hardy Holzman Pfeiffer in 1987, looks down on the view. The River Cafe on the Brooklyn waterfront looks across the Hudson at the skyscrapers of Wall Street. The recently redesigned Boat House on the lake in Central Park is nestled into a Monet landscape, complete with gondolas and surrounded by soaring apartment towers in the distance.

However, such vistas are rare. Most New York restaurants are intensely interior – tiny, long, narrow and with windows at only one end. The standard plot in Manhattan is the 25 by 100 feet originally designated for town houses in the urban grid of 200-by-800-foot blocks laid out

In the 19th and early 20th centuries, grandeur in design was most often found in hotel restaurants such as the pioneering white marble Fifth Avenue Hotel, way uptown at the corner of Fifth Avenue and Broadway (at 23rd Street), where the dining room was lined with Corinthian columns and chandeliers hung from a colourful vaulted ceiling. None of the early hotel restaurants survive. Even the Waldorf Astoria, which was built in 1893 on the site of William Waldorf Astor's mansion at the corner of Fifth Avenue and 33rd Street, was demolished in the 1920s and moved uptown. The grandest late 19th-century dining rooms still in use belong to private clubs – McKim, Mead & White's book-lined Century Association (1891), gilded Metropolitan Club (1891–94) and baronial University Club (1899).

The demolition of so many historic buildings in New York (especially the beloved Pennsylvania Station in 1963) eventually gave rise to the Historic Preservation movement and strong landmark laws. While these have tended to limit new construction and experimentation in New York architecture, they have also provided opportunities for new restaurants to be born in, and inspired by, spaces with a genuine history of a wide variety of types.

During the last few years, new restaurants have cropped up in old bodegas, a garage, old banking halls, an insurance office, the vaults of a bridge, factories and warehouses, and even a meat locker.

Danny Meyer used the Art Deco ground floor of Harvey Wiley Corbett and D Everett Ward's 1932 addition to the Metropolitan Life Building for Tabla and Eleven Madison Park, both designed by Bentel & Bentel. The former mixes Eastern and Western decorative motifs as freely as it blends American and Indian cuisines; the latter, drawing on the architecture of the enormous, light-filled room, updates menus from the dining rooms of the ocean liners of the time.

Hugh Hardy of Hardy Holzman Pfeiffer, who restored the Rainbow Room, the Cloud Room on top of the Chrysler Building and Radio City Music Hall, was brought in by Conran and Partners in 1999 to turn the handsome terracotta-tiled vaults under the Queensboro Bridge (1914) into a two-tiered restaurant, supermarket and housewares-store complex, called Bridgemarket, working with the in-house Conran team that included James Soane (see interview by Helen Castle). And while the decision to tuck part of the larger restaurant under a balcony that houses the fancier one upstairs deprives both of the grandeur that the full-height vaults could provide, it is still a pretty sensational place.

Not to be outdone, Sirio Maccioni destroyed one New York landmark – the festive blue-and-white circus tent that housed his famed Le Cirque in the Mayfair Hotel on Park Avenue – to create the even more outlandish Le Cirque 2000 in the grand salon of McKim, Mead & White's Renaissance-Revival Villard houses on Madison Avenue. The 1882 brownstone version of the Palazzo de Chancelleria (which also houses the Architectural League of New York and the Municipal Art Society, with suitable modesty) had been incorporated into the high-rise Palace Hotel twenty years earlier. But before Le Cirque moved in, the hotel interior had been redecorated, without an ounce of restraint, when the Sultan of Brunei bought the place. Maccioni hired Adam Tihany to add even wilder (and some modern) touches to the gilded, frescoed space on steroids, which is fit for a papal entourage.

It seems the only way to compete is with outrage. In the meat-packing district south of Chelsea, rising-star architect Lindy Roy is turning a meat locker into a nightclub. From the tracks and hooks used to carry carcasses between trucks and refrigerated rooms, she is hanging red leather chaise longues and cast-resin tables, which will move back and forth, around, and up and down to support patrons' encounters with circulating friends. Bundles of optical fibres, charged by an underground engine, will create a light field on the structural grid of the ceiling and spell out the name of the club on the facade. One day, Roy's club may be the only vestige of the area's past as it becomes a different kind of meat market. Refrigerated chambers or not, you have to admit that's cool.

Above
Designed by Adam Tihany, Le Cirque 2000, housed in the grand salon of McKim, Mead & White's Renaissance-Revival Villard houses on Madison Avenue, epitomises the drama and decorative approach to restaurant interiors in New York. This is totally at odds with the then all-pervasive minimalist style.

At this point, the sleek and minimalist Suba, which opened in January 2002, contrasts dramatically with the graffiti-strewn tenements and housing projects on the Lower East Side of Manhattan. Its plain, dark glass facade and double-height blackened industrial-steel entrance door could not be more unlike the side-by-side bodegas it replaced – or the one across the street, glowing brightly, its windows filled with colourful packaging, plastic bottles and housewares jumbled together. But before too long, the trendy gentrification inching east from SoHo and south from Nolita (North of Little Italy) will bring Suba plenty of company. Still, it is unlikely that any place will quite approximate this elegant underworld which architect Andre Kikoski carved out of a series of basement spaces.

This is the first restaurant by the young architect, who was working for Pei Cobb Freed when the project began but now has his own firm. The owner was a childhood friend who guessed right in trusting him, for the place has been put together with a confident hand and an original vision, albeit one that took a great deal of structural reinforcement to achieve.

Diners enter a small tapas bar facing the street but partly veiled by the dark glass. They then descend via a series of open metal stairs, bridges and grated ramps to the subterranean dining grotto or a tall, narrow, red-walled dining gallery at the back on the lowest level. This 14-foot-high skylighted space, located in what used to be the back yard, runs parallel to the street, turning the usual shoebox-shaped New York restaurant sideways. Here, an elevated DJ booth promises liveliness later on.

A few steps up, the mood is quite different. Brick tunnel vaults on the cellar ceiling have been exposed, as have the brick sidewalls in the main dining room, which is surrounded by a moat, lighted from below like a luxurious swimming pool. But here, with candles burning on tables and the gentle movement of the water from hidden jets, the light flickers constantly and irregularly. With the polished concrete floor projecting into the channel, diners seated on subtly upholstered bronze-toned banquettes feel like they are on some strange subterranean pier. There is no place else quite like it this side of the River Styx.

The Park

Testament to the role restaurants play in New York today came when two nightclub impresarios from the West Coast invested blood, sweat, tears, their reputations and $5 million in a series of dining rooms, lounges and patios carved out of three adjacent taxi garages in West Chelsea last year. Eric Goode founded the hip disco Area in 1984, and a little later turned a petrol station into the Bowery Bar, both in New York. Sean McPherson made a name for himself with Small's KO and Bar Marmont in Los Angeles before the two teamed up and started scouring northern California for crafts and curios, which are combined in The Park boldly enough to redefine 'eclectic'. It opened in February 2001.

Two gigantic dining rooms, one with a huge dracaena tree under a skylight, the other dark, mysterious and dominated by its bar, look out on a generous patio through floor-to-ceiling factory windows. This space, enclosed but open to the sky (and on one side to the street), is both inside and outside at the same time, but unlike most New York restaurant gardens it isn't verdant or soft. It retains the edge quality of its history. The eye never stops long to fix on any one thing as it is tempted away by colourful oven-glazed brick walls, funky fireplaces, stuffed birds, Indonesian shell-panel hanging lanterns, clamshell banquettes, black wicker chairs, Chinese lanterns, stained and leaded glass. It is a visual, sensory feast that looks to East Coast eyes like the wild side of California. It reminds architect Laurie Kerr, who grew up as a Navy brat in Yokohama and other ports, of the Officers Club in Honolulu. Parts recall the set of a Charlie Chan film; the whole place could have housed *The Maltese Falcon*.

Furniture in an upstairs private party room (which doubles as the owners' offices) is by Corbu and Mies, and is in white leather with gold plating. The walls are rosewood veneer. But there's a fish tank stocked with arowana, which jump out of the water to catch insects. There's a roof deck, gymnast's rings hanging from the ceiling and an English saddle with gold stirrups. Strangest of all, perhaps, The Park is comfortable, in a laid-back California kind of way – the perfect place, as *New York* magazine restaurant critic Hal Rubenstein observed, for 1980s hipsters to come in middle age within easy reach of the new kids. ∆

The natural descendant of the 17th-century coffee house, the British restaurant has always thrived off foreign ingredients and the cuisines of other nations. **Samantha Hardingham** describes how in London the restaurant, with its proclivity for otherness and inventive design, has become a cultural focus in the present climate where 'choice' and lifestyle are God.

The pleasures of eating good food can only be surpassed by the intrigue of entering a restaurant that has achieved what could be called its simmering condition. In diligent hands, it is the state that suggests anything could happen if the metaphorical heat were turned up or down but is in fact always tempered. It is a room that is suffused with a constant atmosphere of suppressed excitement prior to, during the course of and after service. The experience is an immersion into tastes, textures, smells, noises, memories, places, climates, people, behaviours and ideas for as long as it takes to consume a plate or two, or three.

Jean-Anthelme Brillat-Savarin, in his *The Physiology of Taste* (1825), suggests that 'the man who founded the first restaurant must have been a genius endowed with profound insight into human nature'. He goes on to list the advantages of a restaurant, including, most interestingly: 'that a man may dine at whatever hour suits him, its use to those with insufficient domestic cooking facilities, and the necessity of the restaurant to travellers. I would also add the necessity of diversion, to find a neutral ground where an unexpected mix of individuals can reside in the same room for a limited time and chance upon a conversation'.[1] Gregory Houston Bowden writes in his book *British Gastronomy: The Rise of Great Restaurants* (1975) that: 'As far as good eating is concerned, Britain has never fully recovered from the Puritan's condemnation of the pleasures of the flesh. A restaurant is not so much about the food it serves as the nourishment it provides by way of an environment. The 17th-century English coffee house is a case in point from which restaurants in this country have evolved'.[2]

Coffee houses could well have been where the full potential of the meeting of minds in an informal manner, in public, was first realised in Britain. They served a specific purpose as meeting places for political and literary criticism and debate. Their role differed from the taverns of the time where food played a subsidiary role to the consumption of alcohol. The type of food offered in some taverns consisted of local produce such as bread, meat and pies, and to this day serves to fulfil an international notion of British cuisine: as nothing more than a device to soak up the liquid. Like its successor, the private club restaurant, the focus of the coffee house was on nonalcoholic consumption. It serves also to illustrate how Britain's true culinary heritage is founded on the importation of cuisines from around the world, dating as far back as the Roman invasion which allowed access to a large variety of ingredients from distant territories, followed by Anglo-Saxon and Norman invasions and latterly due to developments in transport systems.

The introduction of new ingredients into Britain may have influenced methods of cooking, but the arrival of coffee in the late 16th century, and the way in which it was consumed, clearly represents a cultural shift in Britain at the time.

The very first coffee house, the Angel, opened in Oxford in 1650. Charles I had been beheaded in 1649 for wielding unlimited and tyrannical power. The Commonwealth was subsequently founded upon a House of Commons resolution that the Commons, as representing the people, in whom all original power lay, could make laws without the concurrence of the king or the House of Lords. Acts for abolishing the monarchy and the Lords were passed the same year. The period that ensued, up until the Restoration of the monarchy in 1660, saw a proliferation of coffee houses. The first ones opened in close proximity to Oxford University, and then followed the migration of graduates to the City and Temple Bar in London.

The coffee house was a truly democratic institution with unrestricted access (albeit for men only), and thus fostered a spirit of liberal inquiry. Any man who could pay a penny at the bar was welcome to drink a cup, which enticed a diverse cross section of society. Intellectuals, academics, professionals, shopkeepers and craftsmen all sat in the same room. A cup of coffee was cheap, served as an antidote to the excessively alcoholic taverns, and its houses offered an environment conducive to the exchange of news and information and for serious discussion, even though they were often little more than a small room above a shop.

'The coffee house is the sanctuary of health, the nursery of temperance, the delight of frugality, academy of civility and free-school of ingenuity.' Whilst on the one hand regular patrons were 'inquisitive into natural philosophy and other parts of human learning', their critics exclaimed: 'Why doth solid and serious learning decline and few or none follow it now in the university? Answer: because of coffee houses'.[3] In fact, these original houses were the nucleus for the Royal Society (founding members included Robert Boyle[4] and Christopher Wren), some of the finest prose literature of any period in the history of the UK, and the basis for the modern newspaper.

Groups met as the Invisible College and the Amateur Parliament, and clubs later established themselves in specific locations. The Coffee Club of the Rota (1659) in Westminster was founded by James Harrington, author of *The Commonwealth of Oceana* (1656).[5] Here, sociability and freedom were discussed: the intensely practical nature of the subjects debated, together with the general decorum and formal procedure, all combined to give this Amateur Parliament a real importance. Its frequenters (including the likes of Samuel Pepys) gathered around a large oval table with a passage cut into its centre for the dispensing of coffee.

Having endured abuse from the taverns (who were jealous of their popularity), a Royal Proclamation for the Suppression of Coffee Houses in 1675 (retracted after 10 days due to intense protest) and a Women's Petition Against Coffee, coffee houses almost completely disappeared by the end of the 18th century. Owners of coffee houses became audacious in their pursuit of the sole right to intelligence; they wanted a monopoly on all newspapers. This proved to be a tactical blunder. Any coffee house that was political in character became a private club (and then a grand restaurant in its own right) in order to temper a growing element of rabble rousing, and others turned into chophouses or taverns. On top of this, the government's colonial policy of fostering trade relations with India and China, rather than Arabia, meant that tea became the nation's drink of choice.

It was in the private clubs that a finer quality of dining emerged in London. In particular, chef Alexis Soyer at the Reform Club was the first to have his kitchens specially designed to be light and airy, subsequently encouraging other clubs to improve their standards.

A new breed of coffee house, the coffee bar, appeared in Britain on the crest of the rock and roll wave in the 1950s, providing a new youth culture with a headquarters, and a more neutral ground for women to participate in a social life outside the home. The proliferation today of American-style coffee bars, such as Starbucks, has forced another kind of cultural shift in Britain – one of indeterminate accessory to a global lifestyle that can appeal equally to men and women, young and old, middle class? ... well, middle class. Branches are located (often in multiples) in the high street, and open strictly during business hours. There is little to tell them apart from a mobile phone shop or gift shop – that is, they are consistently noncommittal in the design of their interiors and equally specific in their design not being conducive to stimulating debate. The duration of a visit to such an establishment has been designed in detail.

Such isolated incidents (or rather urban folklore) as the birth of New Labour in 1997, allegedly from within the fashionably spare walls of Granita, north London's modern international dining room, would suggest that discourse now lies firmly in the domain of the restaurant. The combination of freewheeling speech ('The customer is always right') and a measured code of behaviour ('Waiter, there is a fly in my soup'),

Throughout the 1980s and early 1990s it was considered that the bigger site the better, an attitude championed by Sir Terence Conran in order to revitalise a rather stagnant and conservative British restaurant industry (some say that he single-handedly brought the capital out of recession in the late 1980s). Conran's redevelopment of previously neglected areas of London, such as Butler's Wharf (including the Design Museum, Blueprint Cafe, Pont de la Tour, The Quality Chop House and the Cantina – a variety of restaurants for a variety of budgets), and strategic placement of large theatrical venues or megasites, such as Mezzo (1995) in the heart of Soho and Quaglino's in St James's, gave Londoners the confidence to dine en masse. Nostalgic Art-Deco-based design and French cuisine completed the formula for a sophisticate's great night out.

But if Conran opened people's eyes, it was Julyan Wickham who focused their attention. The arrival of the restaurant as a building type, rather than as the domain of the decorator, was announced by Wickham's Kensington Place (1987). More than any other, this establishment has been the culinary and architectural model for those which have followed over the past decade.[6] Wickham's is a truly urban response – an integrated design combining disciplined architectural elements with imaginatively mechanistic components (the furniture looks too flamboyant to have been prefabricated but the materials and punched-out shapes appear so). The blurring of distinctions between space, craft and painting are embellished at Bank (1997), also designed by Wickham & Associates. In the category of the aforementioned megasite, Bank invited a reworking of the kitchen. The constraints of the site led to a linear unit connecting the bar at the front (the former banking hall) and the dining room at the rear (previously offices and vaults). This kitchen is used for the final theatrical preparations of dishes that have ascended from the more substantial kitchens below. Though Bank's may not have been the first, certainly the exposed kitchen is now a standard for many of London's recently designed restaurants.

The continued success of the few examples here indicates that London has embraced a more metropolitan lifestyle, though not without eccentricities – despite Britain's arcane licensing laws and inadequate public transport system which is unsympathetic to staff trying to return home late at night. This could be supported by the more recent proliferation of restaurants, bars and cafés in inner-city areas previously occupied by commercial light industry and office premises. Districts such as Clerkenwell and Shoreditch, which skirt the City, have become neighbourhoods. Formerly the abode of artists seeking cheaper rents away from the West End,

established in the coffee houses and later formalised by the private clubs, is still thriving, albeit that our social, political and economic climates have changed. As a nation we are politically apathetic and bamboozled by choice. We are preoccupied by lifestyles rather than living. And the restaurant accommodates such a mood salaciously.

The acquisition of a site remains a matter of appropriation rather than new-build, although where a coffee house would have been found in a small room above a shop, restaurants today occupy a converted warehouse, bank, cinema, office building or gallery. Hakkasan (2001), one of London's most celebrated and glamorous new restaurants, occupies a less than salubrious basement, albeit of a new mixed-use development, behind Tottenham Court Road.

Notes
1. Jean-Anthelme Brillat-Savarin, *The Physiology of Taste:, or, Meditations on Transcendental Gastronomy* (1825), trans M F K Fisher, Basic Books (New York), 2000.
2. Gregory Houston Bowden, *British Gastronomy: The Rise of Great Restaurants*, Chatto and Windus (London), 1975.
3. 'The coffee house vindicated', in Aytoun Ellis, *A History of Coffee Houses*, The Penny Universities, 1956.
4. Scientist Robert Boyle (1627–91) formulated an atomic theory which has been the basis of physics ever since.
5. James Harrington, *'The Commonwealth of Oceana' and 'A System of Politics'*, ed J G A Pocock, Cambridge University Press, 1992.
6. Johnathan Meades, 'Making a meal of it', *Perspectives*, Feb/March, 1997.

properties are now largely the domain of the luxury loft apartment. Bar/restaurants such as Grand Central (2001) reflect the international mood of the areas' new inhabitants. However, if we continue to talk of pioneers, the St John restaurant was responsible for breaking new ground in two ways when it opened, in 1995, in a converted smokehouse adjacent to Smithfield meat market.

Firstly, St John reminded us that Britain is an indigenously gastronomic country with a bounty of raw ingredients and a diverse culinary heritage (for certain inherited from a succession of invaders from the Romans, Anglo-Saxons and Normans to those fleeing the French Revolution). Secondly, its architect-trained chef, Fergus Henderson, took a cluster of industrial spaces on different levels and cleaned them out, replacing only the key elements that would

Above
St John restaurant and bar. Architect-trained chef Fergus Henderson converted a former smokehouse in 1995 into a bar and restaurant on two levels given visual and orientational unity by a simple grid of lights hanging on one plane throughout the series of whitewashed spaces.

Right
Originally designed by Thomas Verity in 1874, the Byzantine splendour of the Criterion's gilded mosaic ceiling and marble-lined walls embedded with semi-precious mosaics still exists today. It formed an enchanting backdrop for designer David Collins to add bespoke fixtures and furniture to the modernised restaurant in 1995, under the ownership of Marco Pierre White.

extend rather than transform the remit of the space from the serious production of food to that of generous consumption as well. The simple grid of lights that hang consistently on one level throughout the whitewashed bar and restaurant, illuminating pinkish Old Spot Chops and dark green and deep purple beetroot tops, exemplify Henderson's skill and quintessentially British eye. That St John has a loyal clientele comprising artists, architects and businesspeople alike is not incidental. Neither is the opening of Smith's (2001) around the corner. Although under entirely different ownership, Smith's is an industrial relation on a grander scale. As St John is elegant, Smith's takes its cue from the New York deli, cocktail bar, restaurant above a nightclub scenario – roughly chic and very urban.

Complete buildings are slow to materialise, and arrive sporadically in any architect's career. In Britain, restaurant design provides a test-bed for design ideas that can be executed on a small scale, often with a generous budget and with immediate results. Currently fashionable building types for renovation and conversion include warehouses and power stations, such as can be found at Wapping Food (2000), and provide surroundings that contrast strikingly with decisively modern interventions – the perfect middle ground for a profession that struggles to find a higher plane and for a culture obsessed with its own heritage. Alternatively, those who prefer to indulge their own decorative flair elaborate at the likes of the Criterion (1995) or Sanderson and St Martins Lane, the latest hotels in London by hotelier Ian Schrager and architect Philippe Starck. The former is boldly described as their most radical and subversive to date – remember we are talking about the world of excess and glamour here, not a gunpowder plot.

Perhaps architects, like artists, see dining out as another potential source of work (a painting for sale on the wall), or at least inspiration. The 17th-century coffee house acted as the catalyst for the distribution of information, the exploration of specialist interests and the meeting of new alliances. The image of the architect sketching the inkling of an idea on a paper napkin is a powerful and romantic one for the simple reason that we can immediately understand his or her happiness.

Today, in London, eating and drinking out is universally shared and is on a scale that would be unimaginable were it not for Millennium Commission and National Lottery funded projects such as the Tate Modern, the Great Court at the British Museum and the Geffrye Museum, which have opened up new (covered) public areas of the city and, more importantly, have maintained control of (and therefore a necessary unpredictability in) their own in-house cafés and restaurants. This is what makes them particular to this city, and peculiar.

Grand Central is a bar and restaurant located in Shoreditch, east London. It was designed by Block Architecture, a London-based practice established in 1996 by partners Zoe Smith and Graeme Williamson. New Yorkers would appreciate the subtlety of Grand Central's location; on the boundary between London's creative district, deeply fashionable Hoxton and the edge of the city's financial district. Clientele arrive from somewhere in between, and include architects, designers and new-media types. These industries have produced a new, youthful and well-travelled population which has tuned in to Grand Central as both a reference to the culture of eating and drinking from across the Atlantic and for the romantic notion of its urban habitat. This same generation is adept at appropriating the as-found, and Block used fragments of what has landed as inspiration for their design.

New utilities and interventions are applied to the existing raw space. The substantial, double-height corner site with large windows on two sides is stranded between busy roads. Light trails from cars are emulated in strips of coloured Perspex sandwiched together and backlit, forming the bar and low walls that intersect the space at high speed to disguise different floor levels for seating. A single cast-iron column and painted timber floorboards suggest the building has had previous lives, and provide a qualitative contrast to modified Robin Day polypropylene chairs and the Block-designed furniture in the raised seating booths. The lighting rig that runs across the ceiling feeds a range of intensities of light for different areas of the room, and acts as a notional circuit board for the building, electrifying the mood of the interior space whilst drawing energy from the city outside. Glazed tiling on the walls and floor en route to the wcs in the basement is perhaps the strongest evocation of this bar's us namesake and the building's own tiled facade; boldly utilitarian but humoured by wall-mounted light-bricks that randomly protrude from the surface. The concertinaed timber drinks-wall behind the bar is perhaps Grand Central's least congruous element; although highly textured it is deadeningly static. It appears to be more of a promotional device than of any real use to the bar staff. Block's recently completed Market Place bar similarly avoids bespoke components, favouring a site-specific response that romances the edge of the ordinary.

Main
Once inside Grand Central (Block Architecture, 2001), low backlit walls made from laminated Perspex draw customers into the lofty light-industrial space towards the bar, also made from layers of coloured Perspex.

Inset, left
The corner entrance approach to Grand Central goes almost unannounced but for the flickering red lights above the door.

Inset, right
The utilitarian glazed tiled walls of the basement-corridor approach to the wcs transport patrons to a corner reminiscent of Grand Central Station itself.

Smithfield is London's central meat market, located on the site of a horse- and cattle-market dating back to 1173. Its present Victorian buildings were designed by Horace Jones from 1851 to 1866, an underground railway link connecting to the main stations so that meat could be transported more efficiently. Smith's occupies one of the several meat warehouses that surround the market. Built in 1870, the four-storey building is divided into bays, formerly for the loading and unloading of meat, aesthetically to imitate one of Alberti's palaces. Architects Wells Mackereth stripped the building back to its original timber joists and floorboards, cast-iron columns and brick skin. Damaged cornice details, windows and shopfront surrounds on the ground floor have been reinstated, and a new infrastructure of services applied, such as ducting, steel staircases and lifts. As the building had been spot-listed at the outset of the work on site, English Heritage stipulated that soot staining on the external brickwork be maintained as part of its original character. The architects pursued an earnest approach in allowing the dominant hierarchy of the floors to determine the way their agenda of new uses for the building might intervene.

Uninterrupted access from the street leads into the ground floor, a barn-like space which is occupied by an open kitchen, bar and takeaway food counter. Large refectory tables and benches seat customers for breakfast or substantial snacks and drinks. Customers are required to go upstairs to first-floor WCs, a ploy to draw people through the building to catch a glimpse of the rather more seductive cocktail bar with its red leather booth seating, private dining room screened by cashmere walls and the first of two new bold interventions into the existing structure: a large hole cut into the ceiling to reveal the main restaurant on the second floor. This unadorned archaeological incision exposes unseen aspects of the building and its occupants. Extensive staff quarters are also located on the first floor. Chef John Torode's ongoing involvement in the design process ensured that facilities for staff were a priority.

The restaurant business is notorious for poor pay and conditions and therefore a high turnover of staff. The overhaul of this building allowed for the balance to be readdressed with the intention that better conditions would lead to a more hygienic workplace and a more permanent team of staff. Replacement of the entire roof enabled a new floor to be inserted in the shape of a light-filled, fine-dining room. All remnants and textures of the past are left behind on lower floors as customers are elevated into a new room made up of all things modern; natural light, straight lines, glass walls, white paint and a drizzle of halogen lights. Planning regulations worked strongly to the architects' advantage in that they stipulated that new walls were to be set back from the existing roof line, inviting space for a roof terrace to stretch the full width of the building. A bar and galley kitchen which runs along the rear wall is lit naturally by a funnel-shaped roof light.

Smith's connects with, and makes slices through, the city on many levels. It reads like a script of historical and social snapshots of city life, some accidental and some quite meticulously described by the architects – none more so than the relationship with the nightclub that is its immediate neighbour in the cold-store below ground level. A direct lift connection between the club and the roof terrace invites round-the-clock revellers to take in the view and a breath of fresh air long after the chef and diners have gone home.

Right
The street elevation of Smith's (Wells Mackereth, 2000), its scale and building type clearly identify with the immediate surroundings and the scale of operations of Smithfield meat market. The entire four-storey building can be viewed from various points throughout its height as well as depth and towards a view beyond; the ground-floor bar from the main staircase through the layers of ducting that service the four-storey building, the slice in the third-floor restaurant floor into the cocktail bar below, views eastwards across the roofs of Smithfield market towards the Barbican and from the fourth-floor roof terrace. A section through the building reveals the extent of the basement; once used as a meat cold-store with underground railway access today it is the home of a nightclub.

Hakkasan

Hong Kong-born Alan Yau made his name on the London restaurant scene as the founder of Wagamama, one of London's most successful modern restaurant concepts (see interview by Helen Castle). Having conquered the youth market and opened it up to a more diverse audience, almost 10 years later Yau has acquired another basement premises which is home to Hakkasan: a 130-cover restaurant, a 60-cover lounge bar and a16-metre bar (the quality of a bar these days seems to be measured in metres), all contained within a single rectangular space. Referred to as a directional Chinese restaurant, its direction clearly points away from the softly utilitarian dining of Wagamama and faces luxury, glamour and seduction head-on. The restaurant serves dim sum during the day, and an á la carte menu in the evening, and the cocktail bar remains open throughout.

Hakkasan is as much a fashion statement as a place to eat. Yau's interior designer, Christian Liaigre, is famed for his designs of private homes for the likes of Karl Lagerfeld, Calvin Klein and Valentino, and two of London's leading fashion designers, Hussein Chalayan and Chester Barrie, have created plum-coloured uniforms especially for Hakkasan. These names suggest an attraction to detailed craftsmanship, elegance and, above all, expense. Hakkasan succumbs on all of these counts. Yau's brief to Liaigre was to move away from the stark white walls associated with contemporary Chinese restaurants (initiated by Rick Mather Architects' designs for the Now & Zen restaurants of the early 1990s) with a view to bringing back the dragon. To this end Liaigre employs an edible palette of colour in the interior design.

The atmosphere is set on arrival. Hakkasan's patrons step off of a secluded corner of Hanway Place and immediately descend three flights of steps through a tunnel lined in layers of gently hewn moss-green slate, dimly lit at ankle level by crimson night-lights set into the walls. Once one's eyes have begun to adjust to the nocturnal light levels (this contrast is particularly emphasised if visiting during daylight hours) the layers of light and texture that make up the surprisingly spacious interior are revealed. In the reception/cloakroom area one is greeted by a generous outcrop of pink orchids set against a wall of blue glass, backlit to produce a twilight glow – a brief moment during this time of the day emanates a luminosity known by film-makers as the magic hour. The glass-wall feature turns into the main dining space and runs along the full length of one side to screen, and on occasion to reveal, the kitchen.

Dark-stained English oak traceried screens, carved with mutated Chinese motifs, cage the main restaurant area, loosely separating layers of activity and framing views across the space. Weaving between the screens across the dining area one reaches the 16-metre-long cocktail bar stretching along the far perimeter wall. An angled floor-to-ceiling mirror at the end of the bar creates the illusion of leading down another tunnel, descending even further into the earth. The bar is set against a backdrop wall of the same layered sawn slate that appears in the entrance, thus defining the seemingly carved-out boundaries of the site. Backlit blue glass panels surround the sumptuously coloured lounge area at the head of the space. Shelving in front of the glass supports more intense areas of light and colour in the form of crimson box-lights. The dragon that Yau wished to bring back emerges in gold and red embroidery on lilac and baby blue leather lounge-bar seating. A visit to the WCS has become an essential part of every restaurant experience, certainly ever since Philippe Starck created his waterfall urinal in the Cafe Coste in Paris in the mid-1980s. Hakkasan obliges by providing such a baffling low light level and heavy timber door to each lavatory booth that one's emergence into a marble-lined corridor and then back onto the back streets of London is a positive relief.

Given the large scale of the interior and therefore the need to make a strong and confident impression very quickly (customers will beat a hasty retreat if first impressions are not instantly gratifying), the design exercise is one of atmospheric embellishment. Lighting plays a key role, and was designed by leading lighting technician Arnold Chan at Isometrix. Hakkasan is a well executed, theatrical set design with a quality of global corporate confidence that can withstand tactile as well as visual scrutiny. Customers are transported to an air-conditioned netherworld of cocktails and chui chow dumplings. This is chic London, or is it New York or Tokyo? △D

Restaurant Producer:

An Interview with Alan Yau

The London-based restaurant entrepreneur Alan Yau is the man with the golden touch. The impresario behind Wagamama, Busaba Eathai and Hakkasan, his concepts for Asian eateries with very different price levels seem destined for success. Here he tells **Helen Castle** about his work with John Pawson and Christian Liaigre, and reveals just how important the design element is in every venture.

North of Oxford Street in an area that identifies more with the rag trade and Soho than the chain-store artery that runs through it, Alan Yau's London office has the atmosphere of a fashion house on the brink of a show. It is filled with the overflow from his eateries: clingfilm-wrapped food and drink samples cover every available desk space in the open-plan room and bottles of water are stacked floor to ceiling. In the small meeting room in which we sit is a wall of cardboard boxes variously labelled – 'Hakkasan girl uniform', 'Hakkasan manager's uniform' and 'Busaba Eathai boy uniform'.

There is an overwhelming sense of creative flux. Indeed Alan Yau is hard to pin down. His assistant is talking to him intermittently on the phone about the day ahead before he even arrives in person. He is half an hour late for this meeting and has had to cancel our previous appointment to spend a day with Christian Liaigre, the designer of his two newest ventures, Busaba Eathai and Hakkasan, and his two forthcoming enterprises in Soho: a second Busaba Eathai in Store Street and YauatCha, an all-day dim sum restaurant and tea house in the Richard Rogers building on the corner of Broadwick and Berwick streets. When Yau arrives he places his watch on the table in front of him, giving me the expectation of a perfectly timed half-hour slot – à la US Vogue's Anna Wintour. He is surprisingly reticent at first, modest – even shy.

Ten minutes in, however, it is clear that Alan Yau is happy and comfortable talking about architecture – passionately and at length. This is not what I anticipated, or in fact what I had in mind. My intention in interviewing Alan Yau for Food + Architecture was to express the voice of a restaurateur, an impresario, a businessman – someone who would put design in its place and tell me that despite outward appearances it is just a single facet of a restaurant concept. On paper, Yau should be this man. He spent two years studying business, before leaving to work for an engineering company for a couple of years. He then went back to further education to study politics and philosophy at the City Polytechnic in London. Still not having found his vocation he returned home to Hong Kong to train as a prospective franchisee for McDonald's. The experience incited in him an entirely negative reaction. He did not enjoy being a franchisee in essence – the tight operations and business formula left no space for creativity. It was, however, formative for Yau as he was able to turn what he had learnt to good use. The homogeneity of the McDonald's model was an important counterbalance and thus a stimulus to his own ideas. In effect, this encounter with the corporate fast-food giant moved Yau to devise his own concept for 'nondirectional dining' – Wagamama.

Founded in 1991, Wagamama was one of the most successful and influential restaurant concepts of the 1990s, and almost single-handedly brought minimalism to a wider dining audience. Since Yau sold it in 1997 to Rory McCarthy, an ex-partner of Richard Branson, the founder of Virgin, the full commercial potential of Yau's winning formula has been realised through a programme of rapid expansion. Wagamama outlets have since been rolled out on the scale of a global chain. At the time of writing, there are 11 Wagamamas in the London area alone, with a further two having been opened up in Manchester and Nottingham, and three international franchises having already been set up in Dublin, Amsterdam and Sydney.

Yau opened the first Wagamama in Streatham Street near the British Museum. Within walking distance of the Architectural Association (AA) and University College London (UCL), it was an ingenious and unlikely hybrid, perfectly pitched at a uniquely cosmopolitan student market (both UCL and the AA have a large intake of foreign students). It combined the sort of fast-food systemisation that Yau had learnt from McDonald's with the holistic, ascetic and quasi-Eastern philosophy of its architect John Pawson (as extolled in his 1996 tome for Phaidon, Minimum). Though admittedly waiting staff served customers at tables in Paul Smith T-shirts, the kitchen mechanics had far more in common with McDonald's than more conventional restaurants. Just like staff behind the counter in a burger bar tannoying in the orders, waiting staff initially radioed customers' orders to the appropriate food station (hand-held computers were only introduced later). This meant that food came directly from its dedicated food station and was brought out in the order that it was cooked, rather than being prepared as a group order. The production-line system of service, however, with its open chrome industrial-style kitchens, was completely at one with the spartan finishes and canteen-like long communal tables and benches. And the ascetic approach did not stop at the white-walled and limestone-floor interior. Just like Pawson, Wagamama advocated a simple and healthy way of life. Though most of the dishes were noodle-based – soups and stir-fries – the menu extolled the virtues of each dish in terms of its energy-giving and life-enforcing qualities, one of the specialities being various blends of raw fruit juices.

Yau is modest about his role in creating the unlikely fusion of McDonald's systematisation and Pawson design. He attempts to explain away his visionary role in devising and backing the Wagamama venture at the beginning of the 1990s as someone who came to London with 'nothing to lose'. He regards Pawson's

involvement as decisive. Yau first encountered John Pawson through the Wakaba restaurant, which Pawson designed with his partner Claudio Silvestrin in Swiss Cottage in 1987. In many ways, Wakaba was the prototype for Wagamama. An upmarket Japanese restaurant catering to a wealthy North London clientele, its 'shop-as-shrine' minimalism was nothing less than cutting edge in the late 1980s, setting the tone for the 1990s. Its most prominent feature was a curved sandblasted glass window that defined the interior dining space, a Barragán-style giant doorway and a great expanse of white walls, which must have been startling in the late 1980s.

This is where Yau's talent reveals itself as an aptitude for understanding how a design palette might be applied in a particular context to very different effect. At Wakaba the austerity of the pared-down detailing and elements all combine to create a tranquil sanctuary in which service is discreet and formal. This could not be in greater contrast to Wagamama, where the frenetic jostling is served by a simple refectory design of long communal tables and open kitchens.

Once Yau had commissioned the first Wagamama from Pawson, he found him to be an 'all out proposition who knew in wholesale terms what the look and feel should be'. Yau describes the period leading up to the completion of the Wagamama in Streatham Street as 'an education' which 'brought out the real Alan Yau'. (That is, the Alan Yau who until now had not fully realised that his vocation lay in being a restaurateur and design patron.) Pawson was still at the beginning of his career and Yau was

able to spend hours talking to him in his spacious studios, at the time situated just off Bond Street. It was through Pawson that Yau learnt not only the correct Modernist design vocabulary – terms such as 'space', 'volume' and 'light' – but also how to develop spaces with these qualities in mind. Pawson's approach might have been unstintingly minimalist, but it was also one in which they both concurred. As Yau explains: 'There was a great deal of synergy in what he and I wanted from a restaurant'.

In 1996, Yau followed up on the success of the Streatham Street restaurant with a second Wagamama in Lexington Street, Soho, designed by David Chipperfield, taking Wagamama to a broader audience. It is not only larger in scale – it seats 172 and takes up the whole of the ground floor and basement of an office block – but has a much more central and expensive location. Streatham Street in Bloomsbury may be well located in terms of its university catchment, but Lexington Street at the north end of Soho is in the hub of London's media and advertising industries, as well as being within range of Oxford Street and theatreland. Though Chipperfield stuck to the Pawson house-style of long tables and white walls, the greater capacity and scale of the premises at Lexington Street allowed for a more ambitious treatment. It has a much lighter and more dramatic entrance. There are seven full-height windows on the street elevation. Like Streatham Street the main dining area is in the basement, but here this is executed to extravagant effect rather than through necessity. Part of the ground floor is cut away to admit light into the downstairs, while the rest of the floor is given over to the kitchens, which again are in full view as you walk along the long entrance corridor to the basement.

A year after the completion of the Lexington Street restaurant, Alan Yau sold Wagamama. For Yau, the enjoyment and challenge of his job lies in the creation and setting up of concepts rather than the day-to-day management of restaurants. It is their formulation and inception that delights him (at any one time, he claims to have 10 to 15 ideas on file in his mind, and his greatest difficulty lies in choosing which to develop rather than thinking them up). By selling Wagamama in 1997, Yau was able to free up his time and his assets. He was also able to liberate himself from Wagamama's dominant design identity. By the end of the 1990s, there was nowhere for Yau to go within the tightly defined parameters of the reductivist Wagamama vocabulary. The minimalist style had become watered down and overexposed, trickling down into almost every high street. Limestone floors, Vola taps and Butterfly Jacobsen chairs had become *de rigueur* for almost every shop fit-out.

It was clear to Yau that he wanted to move in a new direction, and the transition from the minimalist Wagamama to the rich décor of Christian Liaigre came in the person of Philippe Starck. Yau had always admired Starck's ability to inject soul or character into a space, summing it up as 'Semantism versus aestheticism'. For 12 to 13 months Yau and Starck went into partnership along with three or four other players. The project was to create a chain of organic cafés, which envisaged a politicised eating movement. However, the partnership was terminated, and Starck turned to a Paris-based restaurateur to open a similar concept called Bon. At around this time, Yau also started working on Busaba Eathai in Wardour Street with Amin Ali, the successful entrepreneur behind The Red Fort and Soho Spice, also just around the corner in W1.

Yau describes Busaba Eathai as a 'mature canteen without an entirely original concept' – but this sells it short. Built on many of Wagamama's strengths, Busaba Eathai also has its own distinct identity, graphically expressed by its distinctive logo and corporate identity, inspired by Thai calligraphy and developed for the restaurant by North Design. (Apparently, it was so successful that before popular demand was met with postcards and chopstick holders that could legitimately be taken away, over 300 menus a week were being stolen.) Though the food at Busaba Eathai is Thai, Yau explains this away as incidental. For him the choice of cuisine was an almost arbitrary decision born out of a holiday in Thailand where he particularly enjoyed the food. Like Wagamama,

the dishes at Busaba Eathai are one-bowl meals delivered at an economical price. Like Wagamama it is also no smoking, and goes in for communal tables and power juices. Service is a little less mechanised and attentive than that of its predecessor – gone are the hand-held computers. Its greatest advance, however, lies in the warmth of the design. It is as if the white walls of Wagamama have been inverted and turned to the dark brown of hardwoods. Whereas Pawson's Streatham Street and Chipperfield's Lexington Street Wagamamas were below ground, the entire interior space of Busaba Eathai is behind a plate-glass window looking out onto a generously proportioned stretch of Wardour Street.

The overtly architectural treatment of space at Wagamama has here given way to that of an interior designer. Its designer, Christian Liaigre, is responsible for the interiors of New York's famous Mercer Hotel and Valentino's headquarters in Milan, as well as the homes of fashion designers such as Karl Lagerfeld and Calvin Klein. Thus the main features of Busaba Eathai are its furniture and materials, which for Yau allow for a more 'organic definition of space'. Liaigre's signature is his use of dark hardwoods. These are prevalent throughout the detailing: the window frames, and also the pillars and beams that support the opened-up shop interior and combine to define the wide seating area. The main focus of the restaurant are the heavy oak benches and square tables, intended to encourage the same kind of social interaction between anonymous diners as that at the long refectory tables of Wagamama. The overall effect of the square table settings is to cluster customers together in smaller groupings, making them appear less exposed and on view than in the light open space of Wagamama. The only drawback here is that diners have more corners to sit around, and couples or small groups often end up sitting at right angles to one another. There is no doubt, however, that given the large space the visual impact of the layout is far cosier and domestic with the main light sources being concentrated above the tables, emanating softly from the hanging watercolour-paper lamp shades.

It is in Yau's most recent venture, Hakkasan, that the breadth of his talents has been fully revealed (for a full description of the architecture, see 'Sit Facing In' by Samantha Hardingham). He has proved his role as a creative, pulling in the hottest talent in every area of the restaurant's production. And he did not stop with bringing in Christian Liaigre to design the interior space. The lighting, a distinctive feature in this basement restaurant, is by Arnold Chan at Isometrix; fashion designer Hussein Chalayan is responsible for the waitresses' uniforms and Ozwald Boateng for those of the managers. To head the kitchen, Yau scooped Tong Chee Hwee and two other senior members of staff from

The main focus of the restaurant are the heavy oak benches and square tables, intended to encourage social interaction between anonymous diners. The overall effect of the square table settings is to cluster customers together in smaller groupings, making them appear less exposed and on view.

the renowned Summer Pavilion at the Ritz Carlton in Singapore.

A theatre director rather than a film director, Yau has not only to ensure the day-to-day running of the restaurant, but also its continuity as it shifts functions and ambience over the course of the day and into the night. There are 130 covers in the restaurant alone, but also 61 seats in the bar and 20 bar stools; these are supported by a full cast – 110 full-time and part-time front of house and kitchen staff. At lunch time, dim sum is served in the restaurant and lounge area, with a full menu available in the evening. On Friday and Saturday nights, once again the whole venue changes gear with DJs making an appearance in the specially designed booth in the bar.

This view of Yau, as someone who is capable of perfecting the concept of a restaurant at every level, specifically the design, is one that is expressed by John Pawson: 'What impressed me was the way Alan had an idea and single-mindedly pursued it – to the extent of going on a course in Chicago to learn how music subliminally affects people and travelling to Thailand because he had heard that Thai soy sauce was better than Japanese. His pursuit of the best was tireless. I saw something of myself in the exhaustive nature of his approach. When it came to the design, he wanted to understand everything. This sort of back-up from a client certainly brought more out of me'.

It is an orchestration which at every point in time hits the perfect pitch, picking up the pace and the required amount of energy as the day progresses, continuing to attract customers from midday to midnight. As elsewhere in Yau's enterprises, though, the overall tone and identity are set by the design. The stage set may not be more important than the play, but it is what arouses interest and draws people in – visually distinguishing it from its competitors.

The trick Yau has always been able to pull off is to anticipate or even create the next trend, to be just the right amount ahead – to awaken interest without alienating his customers. It is this knack that has seen Hakkasan win almost every design and food award going, as it is almost instantly assimilated into popular culture. It has already been the backdrop for a scene in the Hugh Grant movie *About a Boy*. Most telling, perhaps, is the fact that the restaurant is the subject of much imitation with Hakkasan-style screens going up across London's China Town. ₒ

Opposite
Interior of Busaba Eathai in Wardour Street, Soho, London, designed by Christian Liaigre. The warmth of the wooden interior makes it, in Yau's words, a 'mature canteen'. Though a development of the Wagamama concept, it is more of a living room and less of a refectory.

Working Lunch

Lunching, with its connotations of leisure and gastronomic delight, is the epitome of luxury. The reality for the majority of workers at midday, however, is a takeaway sandwich at the desk. **Jamie Horwitz** looks at the way design and catering arrangements in the workplace have evolved in tandem over the last few years to explicitly support the current culture of multitasking. The most conspicuous architectural examples are Frank O Gehry's and Norman Foster's designs for the Condé Nast cafeteria in New York and Commerzbank cafeteria in Frankfurt.

The intimate theatre of a traditional midday meal, the waiting and tasting, the sharing and lingering are all absent when eating alone at one's desk. Grazing in front of a computer screen, on the other hand, is likely to be more familiar and less complicated than coordinating schedules among a dispersed group of colleagues, family or friends. While what, when and how we eat has never been an entirely individual matter, the social norms that make lunch particularly convergent appear to be shifting. The evidence is everywhere.

The National Restaurant Association 2000 survey, for example, found that only 19 per cent of all full-time employees in the US purchase and eat lunch on restaurant premises.[1] The fact that approximately 60 per cent of fully employed Americans eat lunch at their workplace is not a surprise to office furniture designers and manufacturers, or to the booming food service industry. Ubiquitous coffee-cup stains on business papers, the popularity of one-handed foods like pitta pockets, and the increasingly common sight of adults walking through airports with carry-on luggage and laptop bags while talking on a mobile phone and drinking a smoothie, articulate an unprecedented demand for designs that explicitly support multitasking. The same trend holds at home. Product designs like the TV Caddy, a round, three-legged stainless-steel frame that holds a single dinner plate and sprouts appendages for fork and knife, salt and pepper shakers, water and wine glass, a candle, a flower vase and finally the vital remote control, transform the traditional tray-like TV dinner table into a futuristic object for multitasking where the aesthetics of eating while watching a screen are raised to an art form.

Due to increasingly asynchronous work styles that rely on fax, email and voicemail anytime,

anywhere, a social consensus about the cessation of work, which was traditionally followed by a time of convergence among family, friends or co-workers around a lunch table, no longer exists. But this change may go unnoticed. The contemporary zeal for multitasking and easy access to the World Wide Web, broadcast television, radio, videos, DVDs and CDS may obscure the fact that one is eating alone or working constantly.

Eating wherever one works rather than talking about work while 'eating out' has long been associated with the labouring classes. As cities grew larger with increased distances for travel between home and work, the midday break remained as short as ever. With less time to return home for lunch, the market for restaurants caused an explosive growth in 1880.[2] The idea that meals would be purchased near workplaces became a fixed feature, varying only by type and location of work. Nearly every factory across the US had lunch wagons just outside the gate, and today step-vans hover near countless work and construction sites at lunch time. This trend of eating at work has led more recently to hybridised office furnishings that celebrate the intersection of food and work by providing spaces for cups and bottles – including a rubberised keyboard that tolerates spills of most common liquids – and even clothing apparel. These furnishings are part of a larger trend in the design of corporate cafeterias and dining rooms which articulates the longing for an aesthetic that attempts to bridge the fissures, splits and spatial distances in relationships encountered by contemporary office workers.

Responding to strong on-site demand – particularly at corporate headquarters and hi-tech firms – architect-

Right
Computers on every table, eating on the couch or in bed is much improved with an individual tray table. The TV Caddy, designed by Joseph Boron, is available through joeymanic.com.

Far right
A graduate student in architecture eats lunch at his desk in the studio at Iowa State University and later explains that he allows himself a meal break only if he works at the same time.

t v c a d d y

flower included

stainless steel, tempered glass.

11" tall 22" dia

complete with 10" plate, wine glass, water glass, salt & pepper shakers, flower vase, candle holder, fork, spoon, and knife

designed dining rooms, food courts and cafeterias were added in the booming 1990s to companies ranging from Proctor and Gamble Co, Condé Nast and Exxon Corporation to Oracle Systems and Hallmark Cards Inc. In addition to subsidising gourmet foods for breakfast and lunch, which can be eaten at nearby tables or taken back to one's desk, these companies offer special services such as take-home meals.[3] At Compaq, for example, employees email their take-home orders to a food court dinner service called eat@hometonite.com, and Hallmark Cards explains that parents enjoy being able to call D-I-N-E on their in-house phone system to hear the special selections for children and adults.

In addition to these developments the design of corporate kitchens and dining rooms has resulted in architectural spaces that encourage employees to combine food consumption and work in an informal environment that is a far cry from the traditional company-kitchen alcoves tucked away in a corner of the basement, equipped with vending machines and, at best, microwave ovens.

Frank O Gehry Architects' design for the cafeteria and dining rooms of the new Condé Nast headquarters in New York City's Times Square, for example, experiments with a complex and seemingly fluid set of blue glass panels that wrap themselves around individual

Opposite, top
The daylit interior of the Frankfurt Commerzbank cafeteria is designed as a transition between residential and commercial zones in a building complex by Norman Foster & Partners.

Opposite, bottom
At night, the interior cafeteria of the Norman Foster-designed Commerzbank in Frankfurt creates an intimate scale for its patrons by lighting the table, faces and food evenly without glare, offering a refuge for both bank workers and for those who live and work downtown.

Right
For the new Condé Nast headquarters in Times Square, New York City, Frank O Gehry Architects designed a corporate cafeteria that encloses and individuates each table grouping with transparent blue glass dividers.

booths, while simultaneously separating the seating and cafeteria areas. Stylish food prepared for takeaway and grazing, or for sitting and eating with others, is by James Sylvestri, a famous pastry chef who does not mind the apparent contradiction inherent in the pairing of the words 'cafeteria' and 'gourmet'. In fact, Sylvestri describes being invigorated by the challenges provided by a clientele that writes for such magazines as *Vogue*, *Vanity Fair*, *Travel & Leisure*, *Gourmet*, and *Bon Appetit*. The dining booths exploit the convergence of a reflexive visibility – enhanced by a central stage-like platform – and simultaneous isolation from the surrounding space through the use of bent glass sheets that surround the individual seating booths. This inward and reflexive focus is intensified by the location of the cafeteria on the top floor of a skyscraper without street front or daylighting.

The Commerzbank in Frankfurt, Germany offers a contrasting solution in a 50-storey triangular tower noted for its innovative use of natural ventilation and minimal air conditioning. Norman Foster & Partners has designed its on-side restaurant on a ground-floor extension that maximises the available daylight, utilises the main flow of traffic, and thus serves not only bank employees but also neighbouring residents. The cafeteria works as a transitional space which links the bank and a housing project that was part of the same development. This strategic location creates a social node, enhanced by a spatial airiness that increases the psychological distance from work.

The design of corporate meals and eating places to enhance work performance rather than family or social life has a long tradition. Much as the 19th-century factory workers' calories were understood to be related to work performance, the psychophysiology of work performance is evident in cases like business-class meals on international flights. In order to counteract the depleting effects of long travel intervals and to assist in resetting one's inner clock against its circadian rhythm, Delta's business class offers 'ideal performance meals' designed for 'international travellers to perform at their best onboard and at their destination'. During a typical seven-hour transatlantic flight, some passengers may choose a fast, small meal served all at once, which optimises their sleep time, while others drink cocktails and elongate their dining pleasure by choosing a multicourse feast. On both the short and the long menu, symbols indicate which meal to choose for your 'ideal performance meal'. High carbohydrates are 'ideal if you have an important meeting on arrival, and will help you rest onboard and be alert on arrival'. High protein meals are suggested for those who plan to work onboard: 'These meals will keep you alert now and allow you to rest upon landing'.

On the ground, high-design cafés sport additions or features that reflect a contemporary attempt to

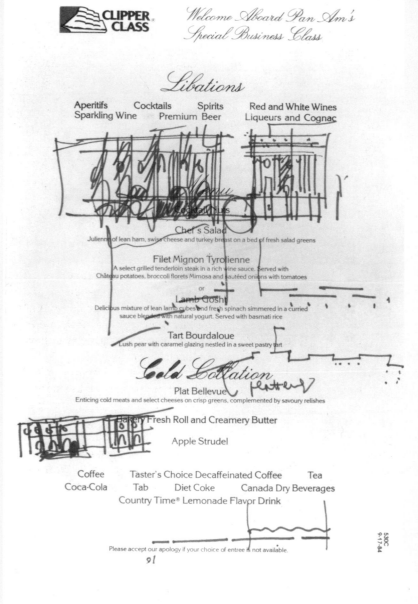

CLIPPER CLASS

Welcome Aboard Pan Am's Special Business Class

Libations

Aperitifs	Cocktails	Spirits	Red and White Wines
Sparkling Wine	Premium Beer		Liqueurs and Cognac

Chef's Salad
Julienne of lean ham, swiss cheese and turkey breast on a bed of fresh salad greens

Filet Mignon Tyrolienne
A select grilled tenderloin steak in a rich wine sauce. Served with Château potatoes, broccoli florets Mimosa and sautéed onions with tomatoes

or

Lamb Gosht
Delicious mixture of lean lamb cubes and fresh spinach simmered in a curried sauce blended with natural yogurt. Served with basmati rice

Tart Bourdaloue
Lush pear with caramel glazing nestled in a sweet pastry tart

Cold Collation
Plat Bellevue
Enticing cold meats and select cheeses on crisp greens, complemented by savoury relishes

Bakery Fresh Roll and Creamery Butter

Apple Strudel

Coffee	Taster's Choice Decaffeinated Coffee		Tea
Coca-Cola	Tab	Diet Coke	Canada Dry Beverages

Country Time® Lemonade Flavor Drink

Please accept our apology if your choice of entree is not available.

91

530C
9-17-84

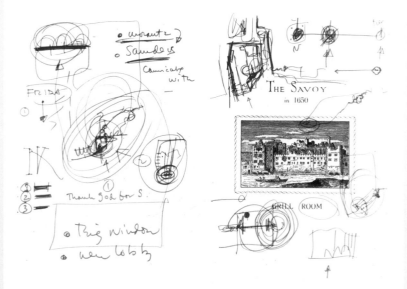

accommodate, once again, the changing temporal rhythms of technological change. For example, in Brussels, Belgium, the capital of the European Union (EU), statesmen and staff from 15 countries travel on high-speed trains, jets and speeding motorcades, first to converge in the city and then to return to their home countries. At the same time, extremely low international air fares have made Brussels a point of entry to Europe for North American budget-minded travellers.

The increase of 'flow' from information, traffic and money in this capital of old-style European manners and cuisine is altering the design of eating in a district where family-run hotels and short-term residences line small streets branching into the massive building complexes where the EU meets. Restaurants in this district display signs in the few remaining pedestrian street spaces that advertise 'Cuisine Tout la Journée' or 'Non-Stop Service', and the same menu around the clock. The flow of people from different time zones, and the odd hours of a temporary workforce which spends much of a week or a month at a temporary 'home site', has produced a demand for food services that is less time bound and more universally available. Restaurants that serve food continuously respond not only to the reality of less stable work rhythms, but also to the needs of international travellers who operate in multiple time zones, fighting jet lag. The convenience of 'Cuisine Tout la Journée' allows people to eat when hungry rather than wait to synchronise their metabolism with local time and local custom.

And there is more than convenience. For an architect of a certain age, going out to lunch is as much a part of the design process as, say, smoking a cigarette used to be. This is not the working lunch with laptops out, caffeine handy and agenda emailed, but a regular meal in a regular restaurant. It is a convivial event, memorable perhaps for a vivid exchange, the kind of conversation that, on occasion, yields a surprisingly synthetic architectural sketch. Because there is nothing handy to draw on, the mythic napkin drawing tells the whole story: taking place inside a conversation, outside the office, in the company of food and drink – such are the curiously productive results of mingling work and pleasure.

Playing somewhere between a 'shout-out' and the 'will to form' Alois Riegl named *Kunstwollen*, the napkin drawing shuttles between idleness and creativity, the perishable and the preserved, and between food and architecture. Neither the paper napkin nor a conventional restaurant is a prerequisite. A menu during a Pan Am flight to Pakistan in December of 1985 can become the site for sketches that show the preliminary thoughts of Robert Venturi and Denise Scott Brown immediately after their first site visit as they prepared for the architectural competition – which they eventually

Right
Near the new headquarters of the EU in Brussels, restaurants appeal to tourists and diplomats by serving the same menu from early morning to late at night. In this district where old and new Europe converge and one's inner clock may not be set to local time, a release from strict menus and meal times is a welcome sign to nonlocal people.

Opposite, top
Sketches deriving from the preliminary thoughts of Robert Venturi and Denise Scott Brown after their first site visit in London to prepare for the competition for the Sainsbury Wing of the National Gallery, which in January of 1986 they eventually won. The sketches were drawn on a Pan Am menu while flying from London to Pakistan for an Aga Khan Foundation conference in December 1985.

Opposite, bottom
Sketches by Robert Venturi on the Savoy Grill menu: deriving from an informal luncheon meeting of Robert Venturi and Denise Scott Brown with Simon Sainsbury during the design process of the Sainsbury Wing of the National Gallery on Trafalgar Square.

Notes
1. The same number purchase carry-out food or eat in employee dining rooms and cafeterias, or describe lunch as a time for doing non-food-related things. See *What's for Lunch? A Survey of Fulltime Employees*, National Restaurant Association Research Dept, Washington DC, Feb 2000.
2. Richard Pillsbury, *From Boarding House to Bistro: The American Restaurant Then and Now*, Unwin Hyman (Boston)), 1990.
3. Paul King, 'Chef gives Condé Nast cafeteria a fresh coat of glamour', in *Nation's Restaurant News*, 27 November, 2000.
4. The Electronic Cocktail Napkin was invented by Mark D Gross and Ellen Y-Luen Do of the Design Machine Group in the Dept of Architecture at the University of Washington; see http://depts. washington.edu/dmachine/fly/res earchPages/research.shtml.
5. Anson Rabinbach, *The Human Motor, Energy, Fatigue and the Origins of Modernity*, University of California Press (Berkeley, Cal), 1990, p 28.
6. Jacques Le Goff, *Time, Work and Culture in the Middle Ages* (Chicago), 1980, pp 42–51, cited in Anson Rabinbach, op cit, p 27.
7. Anson Rabinbach, op cit, p 27.
8. In his book *Non-Places: Introduction to an Anthropology of Supermodernity*, Verso (New York), 1992/1995, Marc Auge proposes the need for 'ethnologies of solitude' in order to describe the dispersed nonphysical presence of others and the unlocatable geography of the highly mobile members of the 'network society'.

won – for the Sainsbury Wing of the National Gallery in London.

Lionised in architectural archives as a form generator, perhaps the least rationalisable in the design process, the 'napkin' has become a feature of 'distributed digital sketchbooks'. Using a PDA-based system it is possible to download the maps, drawings, photographs and texts pertaining to a site, make annotations on the graphics using a pen, take digital photographs that are linked to the text and other data, and upload on-site data for integration and interpretation with a database on a host computer by wired or wireless communications.

A diagram-recognition application of this astonishingly useful system is named the Electronic Cocktail Napkin.[4] Yet the application seems to beg for the next generation of simulation – say the Savoy Grille itself – at the table of two brilliant architects and a generous and sympathetic donor, visualising an addition on Trafalgar Square. Or perhaps if the fully simulated 'design environment' is to include the 'napkin drawing' experience, it needs to supply the benefits of a brisk walk, the sunlight and oxygen, the aromas and sounds of the restaurant, and the invaluable jolt of pertinent questions as well as engaging dialogue.

A 'natural history' of napkin drawing would reveal a lineage from Plato's famous disregard for physical labour and portrayal of a heroic idleness as a gift to poets from the Gods, to Rousseau's *Confessions* (1766–70) where he speaks of the pedagogical rewards of an intellectual sloth between bursts of creativity, a 'euphoric idleness' which Flaubert once called 'marinating'.[5] What Flaubert suggests

is perhaps the importance of valuing time not working. The napkin drawing, then, is evidence of a creative leap that may result from going out to lunch.

Leaving the workplace to purchase a meal eaten on the premises of a restaurant is not, however, how most Americans eat lunch.

Although the presence of on-site or nearby food service at workplaces can be traced back to a period of industrialisation, the importance of maintaining a regular, time-bound sense of work discipline along with prohibitions against lingering go back to the 9th century when idleness was established as a sin by Christian monastic orders. The medieval historian Jacques Le Goff traced the imperative not-to-waste-time to the transition from an economy based on labour-time ruled by religious festivals – governed by agrarian rhythms – to a new commercial economy and an industrious use of time which became 'the new measure of life'.[6]

Modern thinkers from Weber to Foucault comment on the challenge between the 'order of work' with its rational procedures and rules, and 'the order of idleness' with its disdain for the self-discipline and affective repression necessary for labour.[7] In his extraordinary study of energy, fatigue and the origins of modernity, Anson Rabinbach shows that there exists also a long tradition of exception to this literature of reproach, one in which idleness was not only free from disapproval but also venerated by artists.

Without the synchrony, the normative social sanctioning of a cessation of work for shared midday meals, such occasions become increasingly 'special' and infrequent. Soon they could be prescribed as a therapeutic corrective for a creative slump or what Marc Auge refers to as the 'solitude of supermodernity'.[8] Until then, finding the time for slow food and stimulating conversation may be as critical to a knowledge-based network society as the silicon-based processors in our information and communication systems. ⌂

Edible Urbanism

Gabrielle Esperdy explains the importance of the market as a building type. Bringing the city dweller into daily contact with fresh produce and its sellers, the redevelopment of historic markets is an essential catalyst for urban regeneration. An instrument of economic revitalisation, these markets also provide an important alternative, both in terms of the fare they sell and the sort of experience they offer their customers.

As the modern city emerged over the past 200 years, urban space dedicated to food production diminished while urban space dedicated to food consumption expanded. And as the physical distance between producer and consumer increased, so too did the psychological gap between them, until in the 20th century food became an abstract commodity, unmoored from the local or regional. The evolution of food markets, as architectural and merchandising spaces, played a key role in this transformation. With origins in the ancient and medieval worlds, the urban food market ranged from an open-air precinct to a covered hall. The latter was a recognisable building type by 1800, one which symbolised urban modernity and enlightened civicism, especially in Europe.

In the US, food distribution was usually dispersed in open-air markets, though in New York these were supplemented by 15,000 pushcart vendors. The city's food trade was a thriving street-level activity until the 1930s when Mayor La Guardia modernised the commercial infrastructure by radically containing it, banning pushcarts and establishing indoor municipal retail markets. By then, the retail market had already been partially supplanted by the grocer's shop, which revolutionised food trading through combination stores offering fresh and packaged foods under one roof, and self-service stores allowing customers to browse and buy without sales help, turning food shopping towards a leisure activity. Grocer's shops soon expanded into large, self-service combination stores dubbed supermarkets and situated away from old business districts on the urban periphery.

By the 1960s, the suburban supermarket dominated food retail in the US with big box stores, as large as 30,000 square feet. In sociospatial terms, these supermarkets were idealised modern environments; hygienic and standardised in their spaces and merchandise, the sensuality and messiness of food was disciplined by functionalist logic and order. This was as far removed from the public market as the suburb was from the city, with food retailing following the anti-urbanism that characterised the postwar period, when 'new' meant 'improved' whether applied to a subdivision or a supermarket. Back in the cities, this manifested itself in massive urban renewal programmes which often targeted public markets as urban blight. In the UK, dozens of markets that had sustained bomb damage during the war were demolished instead of repaired, for similar reasons. In Paris, the vaulted glass and iron sheds of Les Halles were removed in 1974; they were replaced with a shopping mall.

Market Preservation: Two Results

In Boston, the market known as Faneuil Hall was the original trading house of the colonial city. Along with three Greek Revival structures designed by Alexander Parris (1826), it served as Boston's wholesale and retail food centre until the 1960s. Seriously dilapidated and bordering a large clearance project, the market was slated for demolition despite its historical and architectural significance. When it was finally set aside for redevelopment, the plan adopted was the one that seemed the riskiest at the time – to renovate the market into a market.

Architect Benjamin Thompson and developer James Rouse conceived a scheme centred on 'food in all its forms', including fresh produce from local purveyors along with restaurants and cafés. Non-food retail would occupy the flanking buildings with the streets between becoming pedestrian plazas. Here, Thompson and Rouse introduced pushcarts to enliven the pedestrian areas, bringing the urban market full circle in less than 40 years. The pushcarts reflected the ideas of critics like Kevin Lynch and Jane Jacobs who promoted urban diversity in spatial usage and visual perception, and who would have approved of statements that the renovation would radiate 'the distinctive bustle and life of a dynamic city centre' through forms that were 'non-yee oldee'.

However, the renovation reused many of the market's original signs, and these were precisely what made the Faneuil Hall Marketplace seem so nostalgically ersatz after its completion in 1976. Though it attracted 12 million people annually, as the crowds grew the market changed: while old signs advertising eggs and poultry hung above, the food sellers below were proffering foot-long hot dogs and oversized pretzels. Food remained the attraction, but Faneuil Hall embraced a new identity as a festival marketplace – a touristic, retail environment of calculated sensations and controlled chaos.

On the opposite coast, a contemporaneous preservation project had a very different outcome. Since its founding in 1907, the Pike Place Market in Seattle had occupied a warehouse district of wholesale and retail food halls, restaurants and even a dime-a-dance ballroom. By its pre-Second World War heyday, the market was a collection of undistinguished, billboard-covered buildings that was intensively used and visually and spatially congested. Though activists saved Pike Place from demolition in the 1970s, its renovation was not straightforward because the market had little

Food as Urban Revitalisation

By the 1990s the public market was resurgent, serving a generation with a transformed relationship to food and cities who sought a reconnection with the 'meet the producer' tradition within the urban context. This desire became even more prevalent as reactions against the homogeneity of the supermarket were coupled with concerns about the expansion of agribusiness and the spread of genetically altered foods. Meeting the producer now had clear political overtones, especially in the UK. For urbanites, the burgeoning farm-market movement was also a way to revitalise high streets which, as in the US, had suffered keenly in the postwar period as retailing drifted towards the periphery.

In 1995 the Department of the Environment sought to reverse this trend through the retail redevelopment of the urban core, a position echoed by Richard Rogers in his influential *Cities for a Small Planet*.[1] Rogers called for modest commercial interventions at the neighbourhood level and proposed a London test case for the South Bank of the Thames. By the late 1990s, the regeneration of the area was already under way in projects like the OXO Tower and the Tate Modern. Though poised for gentrification, the South Bank was regarded

as a retail desert, especially in its lack of food outlets. This was ironic since it contained Borough Market, one of the oldest in London, which had been a thriving wholesale food centre for more than 10 centuries.

The 4.5-acre site of Borough Market is a dense fabric of streets and alleys with Georgian warehouses, Victorian sheds and a few Moderne frontages, sprawling south of Southwark Cathedral and tucked beneath railway viaducts erected in the 1860s and the 1960s. As supermarket expansion caused the demise of the high street grocers who traded with Southwark's wholesalers, Borough Market experienced an acute loss of business and tenancy. In the early 1990s the market's trustees began to actively combat this decline by attracting speciality wholesalers such as Neal's Yard Dairy, the respected purveyor of handcrafted UK cheeses. In 1997, Neal's Yard began holding occasional warehouse sales for the public, and other wholesalers

architectural value by the conventions of historic preservation. Prettifying restoration strategies were avoided in favour of cultivated heterogeneity and disorder: food delivery and waste removal in public view; and no stylistic guidelines to foster the existing industrial-commercial character. Exploiting the market's low-life sensibility, including a tolerance of graffiti and drunkenness, became a strategy for ensuring that Pike Place would retain its sense of place even as it was transformed into a tourist attraction. Though mean-streets glamour often functions as the avant-garde of gentrification, the foregrounding of Pike Place's principal function – the buying and selling of local foods – kept the market real.

The redevelopment of Faneuil Hall and Pike Place offered three important lessons about food and urbanism: historic markets could become instruments of economic revitalisation; food retailing could serve as a stimulant to urban dynamism; and the boundary separating food markets and festival marketplaces mediated the authentic and the theme park.

Above
Faneuil Hall Marketplace, Boston (Benjamin Thompson, 1976),. Developer James Rouse renovated Alexander Parris' distinguished Greek Revival Quincy Market as part of a new urban type – the festival marketplace.

Right
Pike Place Market, Seattle (George Bartholick, c 1980)..The Pike Place renovation cultivated the look and feel of a working market and a grunge sensibility. Cheap materials, minimal sanitation and graffiti are tolerated.

soon followed suit. In 1998, the trustees established a regular retail food market featuring Borough wholesalers as well as locally based speciality and organic produce, and food vendors. The success of this venture ensured the regeneration of Borough Market as a wholesale and retail food centre.

The trustees regarded this combination as crucial to the market's rebirth, since it would stimulate virtual round-the-clock trading activity, and was a key component of the redevelopment plan designed by Greig + Stephenson in 1995. Since then, the redevelopment has proceeded at a deliberate pace as the architects and the trustees have balanced the needs of renovation and preservation within a framework of urban revitalisation, mindful that gentrification could easily obliterate the market's wholesale operations and workaday character. To avoid this, new retail trading was sited in disused portions of the market, initially the interstitial spaces between the wholesaler stalls in the main sheds.

Recently, the food market moved to permanent quarters flanking the cathedral, a shift that highlights the market's proximity to this important landmark. The move also allows the renovation of the sheds at the market's heart, including the cleaning of the glass vaults to restore natural light and cathedral views, and the construction of an infill structure that will have as its frontispiece the ferro-vitreous portico of the Floral Hall that stood in the pre-festival marketplace Covent Garden.

Facing Stoney Street and serving as a principal entrance, the Floral Hall portico will link Borough Market with the network of surrounding streets, encouraging their

renovation and redevelopment into mixed commercial and residential use. The portico will also give Borough Market a more forceful civic presence, serving as an architectural anchor and providing an identifiable image within the visual and spatial jumble of the district. It is precisely this jumble, the accretion of centuries of occupation, that gives Borough Market its distinctive character, what architect Ken Greig calls its 'anarchic and conflicting geometries'. As planned, the restoration will make use of this complexity even as it renders usage and circulation more legible. The goal is to smooth, but not eliminate, the distinctions between old and new, refined and industrial, undercroft and open air.

This complexity has an obvious social dimension as well, one that, with the ongoing restoration, must also be designed in order to smooth the transitions between early morning wholesalers, daytime shoppers, and evening and late-night revellers all existing within a single urban district. If the revitalised market succeeds in not merely accommodating this social mix, but in cultivating it, then it may become a model for 21st-century urbanism.

As a blueprint for community revitalisation, the redeveloped Borough Market is a more comprehensive version of a food-based urbanism that has been practised in New York City since 1976 when the Council on the Environment began its Greenmarket programme to bring local farmers to city streets to sell fresh produce directly to urban consumers. From a single roadside farm stand in midtown Manhattan, the council now runs 28 markets set up in public squares and parks, skyscraper plazas, school playgrounds and car parks in all five boroughs. Economically, the programme has kept small regional truck farmers in business; politically, it has improved relations between city and country; urbanistically, it has reactivated dead spaces through the introduction of diverse use and played a crucial role in the improvement of New York's public spaces. In Manhattan's Union Square, the Greenmarket spurred the transformation of a crime-ridden drug-zone into a civic amenity.

Food in the Society of the Spectacle

As a basic exchange between producer and consumer in a public space, the Greenmarkets are the antithesis of the fancy food emporia that are equally characteristic of the contemporary city. Though not unrelated to the great food halls of 19th-century department stores, the contemporary emporia evolved out of the rejection of the supermarket and the gentrification of the city. These are stores that offer the exclusive merchandise of the gourmet or speciality food shop in the self-consciously created atmosphere of the festival marketplace. These emporia effectively combine traditional, albeit high-

Below
Floral Hall at Borough Market, London (Greig + Stephenson, begun 2002). The portico of the Covent Garden Floral Hall will become the frontispiece to a new market building and will serve as an architectural anchor for the renovated market, giving it a more pronounced civic presence.

end food selling with the leisure-time,
recreational aspects of the shopping mall.
Having emerged at a moment of expanding
prosperity, the retail emphasis in such stores
is on superabundance and a profusion of
choice. Transcending the local emphasis of
the farmers' market, they are deliberately
global in their merchandising extent.

The pioneer of this type was the original
Dean & DeLuca in New York, which opened in
1977. Situated in the downtown cast-iron district
of SoHo, Dean & DeLuca represented the first
incursion of upscale retailing that would
transform the scruffy artists' colony into a well-
heeled outdoor shopping mall. The store
occupied the ground floor of an abandoned
manufacturing loft on Prince Street with a bare-
bones design by Jack Ceglic that highlighted its
battered floor planks, pressed tin ceiling and
cast-iron columns. The merchandise displays
were in the same spirit, with high-end grocery
items occupying industrial-grade wire shelving.
Dean & DeLuca's own food line was sold in
generic tin containers and paper sacks – a
contrast to their Lucullan contents.

The atmosphere was an anti-aesthetic with
a deliberate layering of signification: occupying
an industrial site in a post-industrial age, the
store's character was either a nod to SoHo's
manufacturing past or an ironic commentary
on its commodified present. Within the cultural
playground of SoHo in the 1970s and 1980s,
such inscrutability was part of the allure, as
the store achieved a see-and-be-seen cachet
comparable to any neighbouring art gallery.

In the 1990s when the galleries shifted to
Chelsea, commerce again followed art in its
occupation of former manufacturing sites,
notably in the former Nabisco factory converted
into a mix-used project known as Chelsea
Market. The project's centrepiece is a wholesale
and retail market with individual, locally owned
shops lining an 800-foot concourse. In each
shop, retail and manufacturing occupy a single
space, the latter offered as a semipublic performance
visible from the concourse. To enhance the market's
street-theatrical aspects, the concourse is promoted
as an extension of urban space. Visitors are encouraged
to stroll, loiter and even tango, ideally 24 hours a day,
blurring the boundary between the public and private
spaces of the city.

One enters the concourse through a glass and
aluminium grid suspended from an original girder, now
fully exposed and rusting. This entranceway reveals
Jeff Vandeberg's renovation as a kind of architectural
decomposition that accentuates the factory's physical
reality as a collage of different periods, materials and
spaces. Inside, ruptures in the built fabric are fully
apparent, from sawed-through cedar posts to punched-
through brick vaults; this is architecture that wears
its scars proudly. These scars are most visible in the
concourse where they are echoed by Mark Mennins'
industrially inflected, site-specific sculptures including
an imposing fountain – a huge cast-iron pipe pouring
water into a 24-foot-deep well lined with rough granite
blocks. Elsewhere are reptile tanks and upside-down
streetlamps.

In its blending of retail and art, Chelsea Market
recalls the 1950s art-in-the-shopping-mall

strong and crowds spill into it naturally from the King's Road. Once inside, there are wide interiors and a variety of retro merchandise displays, including circular open-top cases. Exploiting a psycho-merchandising strategy that dates to the 1930s, the rounded edges of these cases allow a smooth flow of traffic from forecourt to interior. Lacking the clear differentiation of aisles, the interior is well adapted for the browsing or strolling of the Postmodern *flâneur*, whose aimless sojourns now include the spaces of contemporary urban consumption.

According to Conran, Bluebird aspires only to 'maintain the efficiency of the supermarket together with the specialness of the small store', a remarkable understatement for a project the name of which recalls the pleasure dome of Xanadu. While the market itself occupies only 7000 square feet, it partakes of the same exalted atmosphere as Bluebird's café, bar, restaurant and club. Shopping here seems like a privilege – not the sort of place one pops in for a quart of milk, except of the organic, hand-fed on Kentucky bluegrass, variety. But, as Frank Lloyd Wright once observed, if you take care of the luxuries, the necessities take care of themselves.

That the distinction between luxury and necessity foodstuffs is no longer very clear for the urban bourgeoisie has presented a dilemma for the contemporary supermarket. Though standardisation

Above top
Interior of Chelsea Market, New York (Jeff Vandeberg, 1997). The 800-foot-long concourse at Chelsea Market functions as an interior street, lined with shops. Exposed mechanical systems, old signage, and site-specific sculpture add visual interest.

Above middle
Exterior of Chelsea Market, New York (Jeff Vandeberg, 1997). The renovated Nabisco Factory/Bakery cultivates a sort of industrial chic with its deliberately exposed structure and inserted rough steel members.

Far right (both images)
Bluebird Gastrodome (CD Partnership and Terence Conran, 1997). Conran renovated Robert Sharpe's 1923 garage into a high-end food emporium. The forecourt alternates between displaying luxury cars or luxury foods, both functioning to attract shoppers on the King's Road.

collaborations of Victor Gruen and Harry Bertoia. But here the goal is not to imbue the marketplace with the aura of high culture, but to create a space as visually stimulating as the activities it contains.

In contrast, the expanding food empire of Terence Conran does seek to imbue the marketplace with the aura of high culture, or at least high style. In 1997, with his renovation of Robert Sharpe's Bluebird Garage (1923) into the Bluebird Gastrodome, Conran realised a longstanding ambition to bring together what he regarded as the crucial aspects of contemporary living – good design and good food. The garage on King's Road in London's Chelsea was a witty choice for adaptation into a food market since the qualities that made it ideal for cars lent themselves equally well to food; an easily cleaned terracotta facade; a wide forecourt close to, but separate from, the street; and an interior commodious enough to allow the turning radius of a car.

Accessorised by Conran's own design firm, CD Partnership, in a sleek but not intimidating Modernism, the space now accommodates outdoor produce stands and an indoor food hall. The visual and spatial pull of the forecourt is

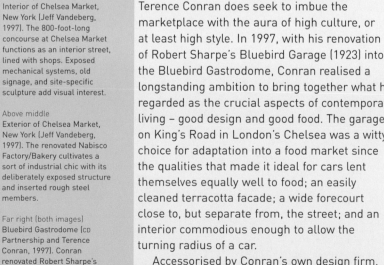

Notes
1. Richard Rogers, *Cities
for a Small Planet*, ed Philip
Gumuchdjian, Faber and
Faber (London), 1997.
2. Richard Turcski, 'Store
design: sign of the times',
Progressive Grocer, October
2001; on-line edn, see
www.progressivegrocer.com.

and uniformity of the supermarket were once a guarantee of quality, these are now a liability, at least at the upper end of the urban economic scale. As a result, supermarkets have adapted the practices that have made the farmers' markets and the food emporia so successful, including organic produce departments, boutique-style merchandising and interior signage to create visual vitality. What these strategies have in common, according to *Progressive Grocer*, is that 'stores have to entertain shoppers in order to survive'.[2] Some supermarket chains are also using architecture as a selling-point – a magnet for style-conscious and visually literate customers. This is a bold step since it means departing from the supermarket's branded public image.

In the UK, J Sainsbury's began to individualise as early as 1985 when it sponsored a design competition as part of a chain expansion plan. The resulting stores use a hi-tech aesthetic, from the exposed steelwork and cantilevered tie-down rods of Nicholas Grimshaw's updated market hall in Camden (1988) to the sail-like canopies of Dixon & Jones' superstore in Plymouth (1995). While the shops are visually and technologically exciting, they fail to depart from the big box/decorated shed concept that

informs standard supermarket design, largely because the architects' work is restricted to the exterior.

This is also the case at Carlos Zapata's Publix supermarket in Miami Beach, Florida (1998). Zapata wrapped a classic supermarket box with tilted planes, cantilevered balconies and a soaring canopy that recalls Miami's modern architectural heritage. The facade also includes a three-storey open-air ramp connecting the main exit to elevated parking decks. It contains a moving conveyor which, like the Beauborg's escalator tube, provides a thrilling view of the city as it ascends towards the roof. According to Zapata, his design deliberately exaggerates the distinction between the dynamic vestibule and the dumb box behind.

Publix is unconcerned with this visual discrepancy since Zapata's exterior serves its intended advertising purpose. In a city of bikinis and buff bodies, where image is everything, the ramped facade transformed an ordinary supermarket into a tourist attraction and a backdrop for fashion shoots. Packaging supermarkets with high-style architecture may bring in the crowds, but it does little to address consumers' basic dissatisfactions with this type of food retailing. What the Miami Beach Publix proves, however, is that contemporary supermarkets, like the new public markets and the gourmet emporia, are now full participants in the shopping-cum-entertainment spectacle that defines the contemporary urban condition. △

Architecture, Yum!

The arts of the *pâtissier* and the chef have, like that of the architect, their historical roots in display and conspicuous consumption, exceeding the most basic human requirements of nutrition and shelter. **Mark Morris** looks at the culinary creations that represent the true convergence of food and architecture: desserts, pastries and cakes that mimic buildings; the 'edible beauty' of Art Nouveau and digital blob designs that are as gelatinous as jelly.[1]

Like a scene from the film *Willy Wonka and the Chocolate Factory*, architecture is merging with food for the benefit of worthy causes and festive celebrations. In 1998, the World Monuments Fund, a historic preservation society in New York, held a holiday competition with the Municipal Arts Society inviting nonprofit arts organisations to build replicas of structures or landscapes of their choice in gingerbread. Yale recently hosted a similar charity night centred on 'Edible Architecture'; notable architects partnered leading chefs to create scale buildings in all manner of foodstuffs including candy, gelatin, produce and pasta.

Dedication ceremonies are increasingly highlighted with an enormous cake depicting the new building. Certain bakeries now offer bespoke cakes in the form of buildings for corporate parties, anniversaries and weddings in the form of, say, a new headquarters or the site where a groom proposed. Depending on size and complexity, these can cost as much as $18,000 a cake – the price of a professionally finished presentation model from an architect's office and nearly as accurate.

Architecture and food have often been related; Marinetti's *Futurist Cookbook* springs to mind.

Peter Collins offered his famous gastronomic analogy drawing parallels between design and cookery,[2] and Salvador Dalí wrote of the 'edible beauty' of Art Nouveau architecture. It could be argued that architecture is closest to dessert in several respects. Cakes and the like acknowledge something special, go beyond mere nourishment and mark an occasion; similarly, architecture is in excess of the essential need for shelter. Ruskin asserts: 'Ornamentation is the principal part of architecture',[3] and the decorative aspect of the dessert points to its link to architecture. When critics deride ornament, they must necessarily condemn decorative cookery as well. Adolf Loos, horrified by ostentatiously prepared meals, declared: 'Me, I eat roast beef'.

A successful dessert compensates for its placement at the end of a meal by being visually inviting. In order to overcome a sense of fullness or caloric guilt, the dessert appeals as much to the eye as to the stomach. This is where the tasks of the architect and the pastry chef converge. Certain desserts can mimic architecture so well that they function as scale models and offer a chance to eat the inedible: 'In most of the applied arts there is a tension between the requirements of function and the requirements of design ... this is not quite true of food'.[4] Scale models are useful because they

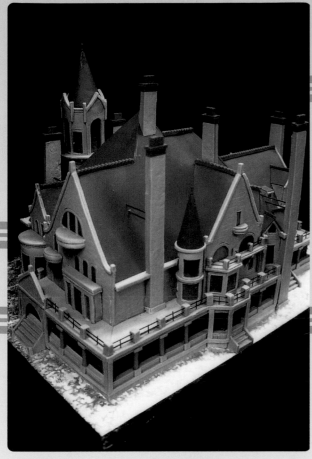

empower by virtue of their diminution[5] – and
what better road to completely conquering
something than through eating it? Chefs inspired
by architecture use the model to fulfil a latent
dream that the world can be swallowed whole.[6]

Taking the Cake

Pastry is largely about shaping forms and
elaborating surfaces. When formed like bricks in
the oven and held together with the mortar of
butter cream, cakes can be tiered, iced and
decorated to resemble any number of structures.
The cake's long history is tied to its supreme ability
to mimic and represent, and this tendency has
precedent in medieval marchpanes. Architecture
and high cuisine both have their roots within royal
courts from medieval times on, both being part and
parcel of display and conspicuous consumption.

No other chef of the period better
epitomises the architectural ambitions of the
kitchen than Marie Antoine Carême, *'le roi des
chefs et le chef des rois'*. Carême served
Napoleon, Tsar Alexander I, Talleyrand and
Baron Rothschild among others. His talents
were in such demand by so many of the

influential that he was thought to be a spy. His
trademark was to produce artful and highly designed
dishes culminating in a dessert masterpiece
resembling an architectural model. These could take
the form of iced classical temples on meringue
mountains or 'oriental' palaces in marzipan with
candied fruit-tree orchards surrounding them. Others
resembled rustic mills with a moving wheel and
champagne sluice. One can easily picture these
delicacies being served at the Brighton Pavilion for the
Prince Regent, a favourite patron, and wonder at the
stylistic parallels between the pavilion and its menu.

Carême, considered the father of French cooking and
the inventor of Proust's favourite madeleine, wrote
cookery treatises like *L'Art Culinaire* and *Le Pâtissier
Pittoresque*, taking inspiration from architects like
Vignola and Durand rather than other chefs. He
famously asserted: 'The main branch of architecture is
confectionery', and launched a trend for architectural
cooking that persisted through Victoria's long reign.

Royal weddings for Victoria and Albert's daughters set
the standards still observed today. The first tiered wedding
cake was produced for the Princess Royal, standing some
seven feet tall and modelled on Wren's steeple for, what
else, St Bride's church in London. Victoria's Twelfth Night

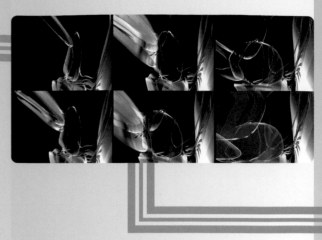

cake measured three yards across and weighed 300 pounds.[7] The 1885 Vittorio Emanuele Monument or Altar of the Nation in Rome by Sacconi allows architecture to resemble cake rather than the other way around. Tourists and locals alike refer to the monument as the 'wedding cake'. This is an international phenomenon: Tel Aviv, Moscow, Belfast and San José also boast buildings referred to as wedding cakes.

Just Add Water

Gelatin is the most mutable and plastic of desserts, capable of taking any architectural form. Standing jellies came out of the English tradition of formed puddings. Ceramics companies like Wedgwood created ever more complex moulds for this malleable delicacy. Special combinations of Victorian moulds with hidden armatures allowed jelly towers to rise high off a table – a wobbling transparent metropolis. The Duke of Wellington's kitchen at Apsley House contained over 500 moulds. Classical architectural motifs were originally the most popular tins. The American Jell-O Company developed colourful fruit-flavoured gelatin and

created its own line of architecturally ambitious moulds, including Art Deco designs and crystalline shapes – imagine slurping Bruno Taut's Glass Pavilion!

Jelly desserts of the 1950s expressed cultural preoccupations with space-age design revived in the digital 1990s with 'retro' styling. Some projects from Zaha Hadid, Rem Koolhaas or Herzog and de Meuron must owe a debt to jelly. A 1950s icon, the science fiction film *The Blob* featured an ever-growing lump of gelatin slowly sucking up anything that got in its way. Architect Greg Lynn cites *The Blob* as an inspiration, and if there is a salient theme at architectural schools at the moment, it is *blobby*. One thing computer-aided design can offer in abundance is a translucency where every virtual building can appear to be made out of jelly. Such projects lose something when they become opaque. Students of architecture know the usefulness of synthetic resins to maintain this illusion in miniature. Casting resin is now banned at some schools for its noxious fumes, but there is also an unspoken aesthetic ban operating here, disallowing tactile manifestation of purely digital dreamscapes.

Nibble, Nibble

Traditionally made only once a year at Christmas time, the gingerbread house is the most architectural of foods.

Above
'Nibble, nibble like a mouse.
Who is that nibbling at my
house?' 'Hansel and Gretel find
the Gingerbread House'
(Arthur Rackman, 1867–1939).

Top right
Victorian house, Greenport,
New York. 'Gingerbread' trim
graces the roof line.

Bottom right
Look but do not touch. A
hazardous holiday tradition:
the gingerbread house.

It enjoys all the decorative options of cake with a more rigid substructure. Gingerbread, formed into spiced cakes or men-shaped cookies, has long been holiday fare. Its formation as a house comes from childhood associations with the Brothers Grimm fairy tale *Hansel and Gretel*. Originally published in 1812, the story describes a small edible house. Two children are lost in a dark forest, alone and hungry until they come upon a small house, 'built completely of bread and covered with cake with the windows of pure sugar'.[8] Hansel and Gretel set upon eating the house until its owner finds them and invites them in. Allen Weiss points out: 'This wish fulfilment, this extreme oral gratification, temporarily assuaging the terror of being abandoned, in fact veils an ever greater and more primal fear: that of being devoured'.[9] A German tradition persists where families fashion their own houses in gingerbread and bring them together to form a whole model village; children are then permitted to dismantle and eat the buildings on New Year's Day.

In successive reworkings, including Humperdinck's ballet, the Grimms' story is elaborated; the house of 'bread covered with cake' becomes a gingerbread house studded with every conceivable confectionery. Like wedding cakes, gingerbread houses became popular during the Victorian age. The association was so strong that Victorian architecture in the US is still referred to as gingerbread. Modern versions of the story make much more of the edible house than the original. *The Oxford Companion to Children's Literature* notes: 'A house built of food, which is the most distinctive feature of Hansel and Gretel, is found in a 14th-century poem in a British Library manuscript, which describes an abbey far out to sea, west of Spain, which is made of pasties, cakes, puddings, and meat'.[10] When Antonio Gaudí built his life-size Hansel and Gretel house as a focal point in his Park Güell overlooking Barcelona at the turn of the century, he affirmed the architect's affinity for the edible building. From its crusty brown walls to its white undulating roof, Gaudí captures the popular concep of the Grimms' structure.

Critic Adrian Stokes wrote of the 'oral invitation of Veronese marble', referring to Ruskin's own wish to 'eat up this Verona touch by touch' after exhausting all other types of architectural analysis.[11] Gingerbread structures permit such oral fixations. That the gingerbread house is often allowed to go stale and become inedible speaks of the illusory or associative value of the highly decorated

Notes

1. The author gratefully acknowledges *Room 5*, the journal of the London Consortium PhD programme, for encouraging early work on this topic in an essay of the same title.

2. Peter Collins, *Changing Ideals in Modern Architecture, 1750–1950*, McGill-Queen's University Press (Montreal), 1984, pp 167–72.

3. Adrian Stokes, *Critical Writings*, vol II, Thames and Hudson (London), 1978, p 316.

4. Mary Douglas, 'Food as an art form,' *Studio, International Journal of Modern Art*, September 1974, p 84.

5. For a survey of the miniature in general, see Susan Stewart, *On Longing, Narratives of the Miniature, the Gigantic, the Souvenir, the Collection*, Duke University Press (Durham), 1993, ch 2.

6. See also Brillat-Savarin, *The Physiology of Taste: Or Meditations on Transcendental Gastronomy*, (1825), trans MFK Fisher, Basic Books (New York), 2000.

7. SR Charsley, *Wedding Cakes & Cultural History*, Routledge (London), 1992, p 75.

8. Jacob and Wilhelm Grimm, *Kinder- und Hausmärchen, Gesammelt durch die Brüder Grimm*, Berlin, 1822.

9. Ron Scapp and Brian Seitz (eds), *Eating Culture*, State University of New York Press (Albany), 1998, p 161.

10. Humphrey Carpenter and Mari Prichard, *The Oxford Companion to Children's Literature*, Oxford University Press (Oxford), 1984; see entry for 'Hansel and Gretel'.

11. Adrian Stokes, op cit.

12. James Thurber, *Further Fables for Our Times*, Simon and Schuster (New York), 1956, p 41.

Above left
Enid Haupt Conservatory,
New York Botanic Garden:
gingerbread cake (Beyer
Blinder Belle Architects, 1998).
The firm won the prize for
'Best Overall' in the
Gingerbread Competition held
by the World Monuments Fund
and Municipal Arts Society.
The glass roof was made from
sheets of melted sugar and
shaped on a mould; the
conservatory housed plants
and trees made of candy.

Above right
Hagia Sophia, Istanbul, Turkey.
Gingerbread cake made by
World Monuments Fund staff,
Christmas 1997, under the
guidance of Jon Calame.

Opposite
The Eiffel Tower, Paris (Mike's
Amazing Cakes). Possibly
Mike McCarey's most popular
'building' for a wedding cake,
Paris being the romantic site
of the groom's proposal, the
couple's meeting or their
honeymoon.

dessert; some are simply too (visually) good to eat, much to the dismay of children. The Grimms' story and *The Blob* narrative associate danger with eating. The allegiance of the gingerbread house to architecture is so strong it seems to refuse easy digestion.

Freud noted that the oral phase was not just about gratification and desire. Concurrent with notions of pleasurable sucking, chewing and swallowing were aggressive death-drive impulses linked to biting and spitting. Here the oral combines modes of satisfaction with a wilful destructiveness. Edible architecture plays to both aspects in a way that nothing else could. In the very process of eating something sweet, a fantasy demolition of buildings is made possible. Primal fears of being eaten are overcome through the ingestion of gingerbread structures as in Hansel and Gretel. Mannerist architects presented the doorway as a giant mouth swallowing everyone that entered. It is only natural to want to reverse that relationship from time to time.

It is a combination of cake and gingerbread house that produces the edible architectural model. That such hybrid objects should receive particular attention now is coincident with a renewed interest in cookery in general, and the decline of real scale models in favour of the digital. The architect, of course, is hesitant to eat his or her own project as it is really a kind of

regurgitation. Having created the building from drawings to models in order to free the project from the intellect and communicate it to the outside world, it is perverse to be asked to consume it – to have your cake and eat it too. For everyone else, however, feasting on a building is a delicious fairy tale, a potlatch, a moment of superabundance. It is an instance of ritual destruction and internalisation of an architectural idea.

Events like the World Monuments Fund gingerbread contest draw upon fairy-tale and bridal associations. These build upon very basic human requirements: food and shelter. Merging the two into food-as-architecture offers a double helping of comfort and reassurance. Delighting in this, such projects typically exaggerate detail or indulge in whimsical expression. That these are expressed in pastry or sweets points to the structural merit of sugar paste and notes their more rarified and celebratory nature. Le Corbusier claimed he could spot an architect by the way he or she rearranged their place setting during dinner. That compulsive tendency to reorder not just the built environment but everything at hand must also extend to the zone of the plate itself. Notions of aesthetic taste here spring from the sensorial. Edible architectural models conjure Lilliput or King Kong just enough to empower and satisfy. Such objects also help to counter architecture's ambivalence about a predominantly visual occupation. James Thurber was right after all: 'Seeing is deceiving, it's eating that's believing'.[12] ᴆ

Design on the Plate

Like architects, chefs tend to underplay the importance of presentation and style in their work. **Karen A Franck** explains how the design of food on the plate involves so much more than aesthetics, generating tension between the importance of appearance and the seriousness of cuisine.

Above
Sea scallops with two kinds of artichokes. Drawing by Cyril Renaud, chef, Fleur de Sel.

Right
Spiced chicken liver parfait with tomato roses. From *The Art of Anton Mosimann*, Waymark (Hampshire), 1990.

Opposite, top
Poached pear tartare, *sablè au beurre Breton*, hazelnut ice cream. Yvan Lemoine, pastry chef, Fleur de Sel.

Opposite, bottom
Tuna tartare with herb salad and ginger vinaigrette. From *Alfred Portale's Gotham Bar and Grill Cookbook*, Doubleday (New York), 1997.

To answer his client's age-old question 'What will it look like?' Alan Kehoe quickly draws a plan on his computer. Later the client makes only one request – for something red. The following week, despite some lingering doubts that the peppers don't really 'go' with the shank of lamb and white beans, Alan obliges by adding julienned red pepper to the green beans, for this is a dinner for eight and Alan, once the in-house chef at Christie's and now a private chef, is cooking it in his client's kitchen. Using line, shape, colour and height to invent his own presentations, Alan is following an aesthetic tradition from classical French cooking, albeit a tradition that has undergone many changes and taken many different forms.[1]

Chefs working in restaurants, for catered events, clubs and private clients, take great care and great pleasure in this visual aspect of cooking. Yvan Lemoine, pastry chef at Fleur de Sel in New York, is passionate about his creations: 'Perfect saucing is when the plate matches my head. A lot of my saucing is freehand, meaning you have some bottles and little instruments but they are controlled by your wrist, by your eye, by your pressure. And you get a certain sense. It's a joy, like you painted something and it came out just beautiful.' Cyril Renaud, French chef and owner of Fleur de Sel, is equally eloquent: 'People can see that there is attention to the plate. I think that is important. It's a matter of showing that is not just a fictive [sic]. This is really an art we are doing'.

As in architectural design, design of food on the plate is not only an aesthetic matter, and this generates a certain degree of tension between the importance of appearance and other aspects. Some in the culinary world feel that presentation has been overemphasised at the expense of taste, that it has become too much of a fashion trend undermining the seriousness of cuisine. This is a concern of Alfred Portale, chef and co-owner of the award-winning Gotham Bar and Grill in New York, who became well known in the 1980s for his astonishing culinary creations: 'The media labelled me as the father of tall food and architectural food and that made me nervous, even though that may have been true. To me it was putting too much emphasis on presentation. I have a great respect for history and what it has taught us and I don't want to be perceived as being trendy'. Portale declared in his first cookbook that presentation is 'by far the least important aspect of a dish (One doesn't, after all, eat with one's eyes)'.[2] This is somewhat hard to accept, given that the design of food at the Gotham is still an outstanding achievement (and so is the taste). Perhaps the legacy of classical French cuisine is not only a concern with the appearance of food but also a tension between form and content, looking and tasting.

The Dinner Was the Display

The French style of cooking that is still so influential is dated to the publication of *Le Cuisinier François* by La Varenne in 1651. However the recognised founder of *la grande cuisine* is Marie Antoine Carême. Born in 1784, Carême cooked for the Prince Regent of England, Tsar Alexander I, Talleyrand, Louis XVIII and M Rothschild, and published numerous cookbooks containing his own drawings. As an apprentice cook, he made the connection between confectionery and architecture, spending time in the Bibliothèque Nationale copying prints of classical architecture to reproduce as *pièces montées*, or large ornamental constructions of pastry.[3] Made from layers of sponge cake, nougat, almond flour, various manipulations of sugar and brightly coloured, they were meant for display, not consumption (see illustration in Mark Morris's 'Architecture, Yum'). In *Le Pâtissier Royal Parisien,* Carême recommends pastry chefs study the five orders of architecture outlined by Vignola, encouraging them to design '*un peu l'architecture*'.[4] Carême adopted other 'architectural' forms of cooking as well, placing food on socles, or pedestals, made of lard and ornately carved. He further embellished dishes with numerous ornamental silver skewers laced with truffles, crayfish and other items.

Carême's *pièces montées* were by no means the only form of display on the table. At the time, following the *service à la française*, a formal dinner consisted of three or four parts. The great many different dishes that comprised each part were all placed on the table at once; guests served themselves and helped each other. The

placement of dishes of different sizes and shapes followed very precise geometric and often symmetrical arrangements, such as three roast dishes along the centre of the table with two salads and two sauces on each side.[5] Carême's book *Le Maître d'Hôtel Français* is full of directions and illustrations of plans for arranging dishes on the table. Since the French had invented special containers for their new foods, the dinner table could display an extravagant collection of silver tureens, sauce boats and serving dishes, as well as elaborately decorated food. Calling this 'notre service moderne' Carême praised its elegance and sumptuousness and noted its lack of confusion and disorder.[6] The food, however, did not remain hot and some felt the displays were too ostentatious. In the mid-19th century a student of Carême, Félix Urbain-Dubois, helped bring *service à la russe* to France; dishes were presented one after another in sequence, thus remaining hot and keeping their flavour. Servants served each guest individually.[7] Elaborately constructed cold dishes, often in aspic, could still be used as display.

The next chef to shape French professional cooking in a significant manner was Auguste Escoffier. Born in 1846, chef at the sumptuous Savoy and Carlton hotels in London and consultant to the establishment of kitchens in luxury hotels in many parts of the world, Escoffier spread French *haute cuisine*. His *Le Guide Culinaire* (1901), translated into many languages, is still a culinary bible, and his streamlining of the professional kitchen into interdependent stations, each responsible for a type of operation rather than a complete dish, is still in evidence today. Trained in the 19th-century tradition of ornately crafted dishes, and having written his first book on the making of inedible wax flowers for decorating food, it was difficult for Escoffier to adopt a less elaborate style of presentation, something that was vehemently encouraged by the chef and writer Prosper Montagné and was eventually required by the smaller size of restaurant tables and the shorter time patrons spent eating. 'Less elaborate' is purely relative, however, and Escoffier did mount cold dishes on socles made of solid ice, lit from within by electric lights. The first *pêche Melba* was placed between the wings of a swan carved from ice and covered with spun sugar.[8]

After Escoffier, French *haute cuisine* still required finely crafted garnishes. Attention in classic French cooking to the elaborate display of food is evident in its vocabulary. Some of the terms and the practices named are still in use: *brunoise* refers to vegetables cut into half-inch cubes; *julienne* means very thinly sliced vegetables; *buisson* is an arrangement of food, such as asparagus or shellfish, in a pyramid; *vandyke* means to embellish the decorative feature of a dish, referring often to lemons, tomatoes or orange halves with their edges cut into zigzags; *historier* refers to a particular way of cutting lemons into basket shapes or fluting mushroom caps. *Mignonette*, *pommes château* and

Top
The use of *atelets* (skewers), after Carême. From Prosper Montagné, *Larousse Gastronomique*, Libraire Larousse (Paris), 1938.

Middle
Buisson de petits homards, sur socle. Hand-coloured lithograph from Félix Urbain-Dubois and Emile Bernard, *La Cuisine Classique* (Paris), 1868.

Bottom
Dessin 196 and Dessin 197. Hand-coloured lithograph from Félix Urbain-Dubois and Emilie Bernard, *La Cuisine Classique*.

Top
Aspic de blanc de volailles.
From Prosper Montagné,
Larousse Gastronomique,
Libraire Larousse (Paris),
1938.

Middle
Aspic de langouste. From
Prosper Montagné, *Larousse
Gastronomique.*

Bottom
*De haut en bas: Turbotine
reine pédauque, filet de sole
Joinville et Trancon de
saumon glacée à la
Parisienne.* From Prosper
Montagné, *Larousse
Gastronomique.*

pommes Pont Neuf all name different cuts of potatoes. *Quenelles* are moulded, elongated balls of forcemeat; the term is now used to refer to the same shape of puréed vegetables, ice cream, sorbet or any other soft, malleable ingredient. There is even a term for arranging food attractively on a serving dish – *dresser*.[9]

In France, from Carême onwards, many chefs who wrote books and articles proclaimed the need to simplify French cuisine both in content and appearance (the phrase '*nouvelle cuisine*' was frequently invoked) but many conventions for displaying foods remained well into the 20th century. In the 1960s, chef and owner Henri Soulé of Le Pavilion in New York still insisted on the strictest interpretation of *service à la russe*: when chicken or duck was ordered, the whole bird had to be presented to the diners before it was carved, and Soulé himself often did the carving in view of the diners.[10]

In 1961, when the founder of the Lutece restaurant in New York interviewed Chef Andre Soltner in Paris, he viewed Soltner's sculptures composed of sheeps' fat mixed with wax, which were still considered part of a professional chef's credentials. In his *La Grande Cuisine Illustrée* (1900), Montagné expressed his disdain for socles, borders and sculptures of wax or fat, and in the first edition of *Larousse Gastronomique* (1938) he recommended that modern service and modern taste required other concepts of *dressage*. He rejected ornamental silver skewers for decoration yet these appear prominently in his illustrations of shrimp salad and *poularde Lamberty* (these are fewer and less heavily laden than those in Carême's drawings).[11] One could say that it was only with *nouvelle cuisine*, yet another stage in the simplification of French cooking, that Montagné's admonition that all be edible was truly followed.

The Plate Is the Display

Nouvelle cuisine, a way of cooking that emerged in the 1960s in the work of French chefs Paul Bocuse, Jean and Pierre Troisgros, Michel Guerard and others, was championed and codified by two food critics, Henri Gault and Christian Millau, in 1973. Among other defining characteristics, this style of cooking reduced cooking time, emphasised the use of the freshest ingredients, eliminated rich sauces and encouraged inventiveness.[12] It also stressed visual presentation, not with elaborately cut garnishes or inedible decorations but with the food itself, food that was artistically arranged in small portions, not on platters or in serving bowls, but on large, individual plates. This remains the predominant approach to presentation in many restaurants and catered events today. Sauces no longer hide the food by covering it but are often placed beneath or next to the food, thus both revealing it and forming striking patterns. The sauce may be 'pulled': a little dot is placed on the plate and is 'pulled' with a toothpick, or several different coloured sauces may be used like paint. With the adoption of *service à l'assiette*, chefs in the kitchen, and not waiting

staff, became responsible for the appearance of individual plates. Earlier forms of service presented the diner with entire dishes or several individual servings on a platter, and waiting staff served the portions, arranging the food on each plate.

The studied arrangement of a few items of food on a single plate, with attention to the colour and texture of the food and the surrounding space, indicates the influence of Japanese cooking on *nouvelle cuisine*. French chefs visited Japan, particularly during the Tokyo Olympics of 1964, and brought ideas home with them.[13] Anton Mosimann, once chef at the Dorchester in London and now caterer by appointment to the Prince of Wales, was one of the first chefs in England

> The studied arrangement of a few items of food on a single plate, with attention to the colour and texture of the food and the surrounding space, indicates the influence of Japanese cooking on *nouvelle cuisine*.

to adopt a style similar to *nouvelle cuisine*. He reports that his one-year stay in Japan in the 1970s strongly influenced his cooking: he learned about presentation, simplicity, freshness.

The freedom from classical French conventions sparked by *nouvelle cuisine* encouraged chefs to invent their own dishes as well as artful presentations of them. In the past both the content of the dish and how it should be garnished and arranged on the plate had been dictated. Now all kinds of possibilities are pursued. When he joined the Gotham Bar and Grill in 1985 after working for a year in France, Alfred Portale noted that 'food was flat'. Thinking about the different styles of bonsai trees he had studied, where the branches form triangles, and possibly drawing upon his experience as a jeweller, Portale began to build food up, lifting it off the plate to give it 'dimension and air' and creating different levels. Still using this approach, Portale also wants the food to 'look natural' and decries some chefs 'torturing' food by baking it in copper pipes or placing it on bathroom tiles. Cyril Renaud, who opened the Fleur de Sel in 2000, and whose paintings grace the walls, menus and business cards of the restaurant, has no doubt that 'the first thing you do is eat the food with your eyes. I do as well'. He stresses simplicity: 'I use my imagination to have something that makes sense, that doesn't confuse people ... It has to be beautiful and simple and striking right away'.

Marcus Samuelsson, executive chef and co-owner of Acquavit in New York, is also a painter. He is well aware

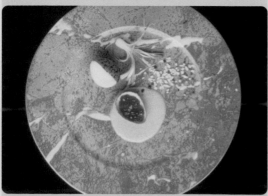

Top
Raspberry *feuilleté*, white chocolate caramel *ganache*. Yvan Lemoine, pastry chef, Fleur de Sel.

Right, top
Chocolate mouse with white and dark chocolate sauces. From *The Art of Anton Mosimann*, Waymark (Hampshire), 1990.

Right, bottom
Gull's egg served on a watercress sauce with salmon caviar. From *The Art of Anton Mosimann*.

Opposite, top
Salmon with beet sorbet, potato and black mustard. Marcus Samuelsson, chef, Acquavit.

Opposite, bottom
Grilled soft-shell crabs with Israeli couscous and summer vegetable sauté. From *Alfred Portale's 12 Seasons Cookbook*, Broadway Books (New York), 2000.

of his restaurant's proximity to MOMA and is inspired by artists and designers, particularly Jackson Pollock and Jasper Johns. From his first day at Acquavit, he stocked the kitchen with brushes, and relishes using a variety of unusual plates, including glass block, large and small. As he demonstrates painting black mustard next to a serving of smoked salmon, with the stroke crossing the square plate's rim, he comments: 'You work with negative space. You open up the dish. You have to go over the rim. Otherwise it wouldn't be seen'. Alan Kehoe points out that design on the plate is not a 'highly evolved art. It's mostly lines, triangles, squares and circles. You still have to have a very good spatial sense'. With *service à l'assiette* the plate must look pretty. This is hard to do with the traditional beef Wellington requested by a client, so Alan deconstructed it: 'I made the puff pastries separate in little triangles. There's the beef fillet; underneath is the Bordelaise sauce and there are three little piped towers of the liver'.

Constraints and Opportunities

Like architecture and unlike painting or sculpture, cooking is an 'operative art' with its own constraints.[14] In fact, Portale reports that it was just such constraints that helped inspire his tall food. He needed fish to cook quickly: by cutting a large piece of bass into two pieces and cooking them on top of the stove he could reduce cooking time from 12 minutes to three. He plated the slices on top of one another and so began to stack food. In order to prevent things from sliding, he 'often put down braised chard or a little bed of vegetables underneath things'. Some ingredients have a good high performance factor, or hpf, on the plate: 'They stack well, they're neat, you can control their size and shape'. Uniformity of size and shape is also important. Portale invented a dish of pan-roasted sweetbreads, roasted porcini mushrooms and a quenelle of parsnip purée. While it was delicious, the size of the porcinis was inconsistent and after watching the 'plates go out really sloppy or messy, I had to take it off [the menu]'.

Consistency across dishes, in the arrangement of food and the size and shape of each item, is key. Restaurants will keep drawings of dishes on file for this reason, and chefs who take the Certified Master Chef exam at the Culinary Institute of America are graded on both their skill in slicing and the consistency of the slices.[15]

How far the dish must travel from the kitchen, and how many people handle it, are also factors to consider. When Renaud was executive chef at La Caravelle, this was an important constraint: the dining room was 50 yards from the kitchen, as well as up a flight of stairs, and each dish was handled by four people before it reached the table. In Cyril's own restaurant, the kitchen is immediately adjacent to the dining room, and only one waiter handles each plate – not even the chef touches it. Waiting staff at the Gotham, however, must carry the food upstairs, and rumour has it that one station is known as the spot for

repairing presentations. Portale acknowledges this, but does not sanction the practice out of some concern that waiting staff may not always be sufficiently skilled in repairing. Out of 300 dinners a night, 15 or 20 plates need repairing even before they leave the kitchen simply because ingredients slip or don't look right.

Since, unlike art, the food so beautifully designed will be eaten, the process of doing so becomes another consideration. Eric Mongno, the *sous-chef* at Fleur de Sel, points out that 'you want to be able to eat some and it still maintains its shape and form, so it's still pleasing to the eyes as you eat it and it's not just mish-mash'. One example Portale gives is a *millefeuille*: if the layers are too thick or the pastry is too sturdy, 'when you hit it with a spoon, the whole thing will smoosh'. The layers have to be thin enough for the spoon to just 'crack through it'.

The process of eating also suggests how the plate should be oriented to the diner. Waiters are directed how to place the plate according to hands on the clock: green beans at six o'clock. According to Anton Mosimann, the standard in classical cuisine was for the main dish to face the diner with the starch to the left, at 10 to 12, and the vegetables to the right, at 10 past 12. With or without this standard, the meal must be easy to eat, so, for instance, meat and other food that requires cutting will still be placed towards the front, closest to the diner.

Top
Autumn salad of pears, gorgonzola and walnut vinaigrette. From *Alfred Portale's 12 Seasons Cookbook*, Broadway Books (New York), 2000.

Right
Belon and Wellfleet oysters, tomato lime mint tea, spring peas and fava beans. Cyril Renaud, chef, Fleur de Sel.

Slipping and sliding is always a concern with certain kinds of foods, like peas, so Portale mixes sliced pearl onions with them. Similarly, sorbet has to be placed on something because as it melts it will slide. What started as a functional requirement can enhance its appearance, so 'you put the sorbet on a little disc of meringue or a little pile of nuts, or you make a little cup out of *tuille* and then maybe the *tuille* wraps around and points up and that pulls the design of the dish together'. In addition there is the age-old problem of temperature. If a warm dish is too high off the plate it will loose the heat provided by the plate.

As shown here, from the days of Carême onwards the most elaborately designed dishes are often cold foods and desserts. In each case, handling and decorating can be done without fear of the dish getting cold (although desserts may melt). Frequently, desserts are still the most intricate of dishes; in large restaurants as many as three kitchen staff may work on one order. For both appetisers and desserts, the amount of food served is less than that for the main courses, giving the chef more space on the plate to work with.

It does not seem to be by chance that seafood figures prominently in these pictures, from the past and the present. Perhaps this is because of its festive connotations and because, as Portale notes, it has such great variety and flexibility, giving it more 'creative possibilities' than meat or poultry.[16]

Design Choices
As much as the design of the food is a painting, the plate itself is the canvas and the frame. It is important to many contemporary chefs that there is sufficient space around the food, hence what seem to be, from a domestic point of view, the use of excessively large plates for main courses as well as hors d'oeuvres and desserts. Alan Kehoe speculates that as food became smaller with the emergence of *nouvelle cuisine*, chefs began 'seeing the food with space and then started saying, "Well, I can also make a bigger plate and that will give me more space to play with". I know that happened with me'.

Renaud is explicit regarding the painting analogy: 'I like to have the white. It's like a painting to me. The white gives me the sense that I can play with the colours'. The white and the size of the plate 'make it a little more open. It gives more sense of breathing. It's not so stressful. I don't want my food to be looking stressful'. Marcus Samuelsson refers to the stress of the contemporary world outside the restaurant: 'The eye needs something to rest on. We live in

a CNN and MTV world where we get information so fast. I feel in this space, in here, we should not'.

The proportion of food to plate and the geometrical relationships to be created are what guide design choices. Portale scales food up or down to fit a certain plate or a certain occasion. Preferring plates with a rim, he finds the rim sacrosanct. Asked if he ever places food on the rim, he laughs, 'Never. You're not supposed to have food on the rim of the plate'. Similarly, *sous-chef* Eric Mongno at Fleur de Sel feels that certain plate presentations 'are out of control. Saucing all over the plate and decorating the rims doesn't really enhance the food'.

Portale likes to work with odd numbers, such as three, five or seven. Often working with three components, he tends to centre them, which works best on a round plate; with an oval plate, he will place two foods opposite each other. Symmetry and balance are paramount. Yvan, pastry chef at Fleur de Sel, acknowledges that he tries to be a perfectionist. On a square plate he prefers to put four quenelles of sorbet, placing them very carefully so that they line up with the corners, with the fatter side of the quenelle to the right of the diner. As all chefs do, Yvan plans the composition with the plate's orientation to the diner in mind: 'If there is something special, like ice cream, it is always at two, three o'clock', possibly with a chocolate tart in the middle. In the banana dessert, the chocolate dots start at two, three o'clock: 'At the top you

Right, top
Soft shell crab, dusted with almond flour, with pea emulsion. Cyril Renaud, chef, Fleur de Sel.

Right, bottom
Double rack of lamb, spring vegetable tian and tomato jam. Cyril Renaud, chef, Fleur de Sel.

really don't see it. At the bottom it is too constricting. At the side it gets left out'.

Today plates are not always round, nor do all the plates on a table have to match. There is a growing variety including shallow bowls and plates of different shapes and materials (though there is not much experimentation with colour, with the exception of Mosimann). They are, however, always spacious; if small plates are used, it is only because there is a series of them, all sitting on a larger plate, as at Acquavit. The variety of plates and the attention to which plate is best for which dish is reminiscent of Japanese cuisine, where plates are chosen to complement the dishes, to reflect the season or to follow a theme.

There seems to be much more playfulness in Western cuisine today and chefs may be inspired by a particular plate to create a dish especially for it. For *The Art of Anton Mosimann*, Mosimann selected 50 plates and then created a dish for each, exclusively for inclusion in the book. Cyril Renaud and Yvan often drop by the porcelain shop of Villeroy & Boch to look at plates. According to Yvan: 'We love going there. We see a new plate and it plays so well. It's a certain magic that really happens from looking at the plate'. A square, rugged glass plate became a favourite for serving brightly coloured fruits like roasted apricots. Fleur de Sel now has about 50 different kinds of plates;

sometimes there are only one or two of a particular kind, which may be used for a special order from a customer with dietary restrictions or for a tasting menu of desserts.

One unusual plate at Fleur de Sel is an extended, oblong shape made of metal. At Acquavit, a similarly shaped plate of heavy glass was made to order for Chef Samuelsson, joining an amazing array of plates at Acquavit including oval ones made entirely from sugar. Marcus Samuelsson was born in Ethiopia. Adopted by a Swedish couple, he grew up in Sweden, trained in France and now lives in New York. With this background and a spirit of adventure, he seems unconstrained by culinary conventions. When asked about 'regular plates', he responds: 'We do serve on regular plates but what is "regular"? I can tell you the French guy or the Luxembourg guy didn't have me in mind when they made the plate. When I cook for you at my house, the food is about my cooking for you. A restaurant is a thousand times that'.

Samuelsson chose the glass block with the thought that midtown restaurants should not become too stiff and boring. Also, 'by putting this glass block out at the beginning of dinner, I know everybody will have excitement. People are awake right away. This gives a kick. It forces people to communicate, to converse over food'. Travelling frequently in Asia and Africa, Samuelsson discovers plates made of reeds or bread.[17] He is now designing his own porcelain plate, shaped like a boat, to be manufactured in Sweden. Calling himself a global citizen,

Right
Oysters with caviar, mango sorbet and cucumber jelly. Marcus Samuelsson, chef, Acquavit.

Inset
Gravlax with quail egg. Marcus Samuelsson, chef, Acquavit.

Opposite, top
Seared tuna with caponata, pappardelle and red wine sauce. From *Alfred Portale's Gotham Bar and Grill Cookbook*, Doubleday (New York), 1997.

Opposite, bottom
Guide to Gotham presentation of seared tuna. From *Alfred Portale's Gotham Bar and Grill Cookbook*.

Notes
1. The focus of this article is arranging food on the plate. For a discussion of the design of items of food, particularly pasta, see Paola Antonelli 'Design bites', in Claire Catterall (ed) *Food Design and Culture*, Laurence King (London), 1999, and Antonelli's forthcoming book.
2. Alfred Portale, *Gotham Bar and Grill Cookbook*, Doubleday (New York), 1997, p 25.
3. Stephen Mennell, *All Manners of Food: Eating and Taste in England and France from the Middle Ages to the Present*, University of Illinois Press (Urbana), 1996.
4. MA Carême, *Le Pâtissier Royal Parisien*, Au Dépôt de Libraire (Paris), 1854, p 2.
5. Prosper Montagné, *Larousse Gastronomique*, Clarkson Potter (New York), 2001.
6. MA Carême, *Le Maître d'Hôtel Français*, Didot (Paris), 1822.
7. Ann Eatwell, 'À la française to à la russe, 1680-1930', in Philippa Glanville and Hilary Young (eds) *Elegant Eating: Four Hundred Years of Dining in Style*, V & A Publications (London), 2002.
8. Timothy Shaw, *The World of Escoffier*, The Vendome Press (New York), 1995.
9. Montagné, op cit. See also May B Trubek, *Haute Cuisine: How the French Invented the Culinary Profession*, University of Pennsylvania Press (Philadelphia), 2000.
10. Patrick Kuh, *The Last Days of Haute Cuisine: The Coming of Age of American Restaurants*, Penguin (New York), 2001.
11. Prosper Montagné, *Larousse Gastronomique*, Librairie Larousse (Paris), 1938.
12. Mennell, op cit.
13. Jean-Robert Pitte, *French Gastronomy*, trans Jody Gladding, Columbia University Press (New York), 2002.
14. Witold Rybczynski, *The Look of Architecture*, Oxford University Press (New York), 2000.
15. Michael Ruhlman, *The Soul of a Chef*, Penguin (New York), 2001.
16. Portale, op cit. p 180.
17. Thick slices of bread served as plates in England until the 16th century, when they were replaced by thick wooden platters (Hazel Forsyth, 'Trenchers and porringers in Europe', in Glanville and Young, op cit). In Italy the transition took place much earlier, in the 12th century, when both wood and terracotta were used (Giovanni Rebora, *The Culture of the Fork*, trans Albert Sonnenfeld, Columbia University Press (New York), 2001).

he finds 'tradition' not just in Europe but across the whole world, commenting that: 'The evolution of the plate is never ending. It can end only if we confine it to Europe and to France. If you use the rest of the world as a starting point, then you're not going to end'.

Design at Home

While not everyone who cooks is a chef, everyone who cooks does place food on a plate – a serving plate or an individual plate. To this extent we are all designing food on the plate. Unlike the extremely costly, time-consuming and highly specialised techniques required for the presentations invented by Marie Antoine Carême, Félix Urbain-Dubois or Auguste Escoffier, the plating style common among contemporary chefs like Alfred Portale or Cyril Renaud can be approximated at home. In this way the design of food in many restaurants today is more democratic, as well as more edible, than that of previous traditions. In his first cookbook, Portale gives directions for 'everyday presentations' and 'Gotham presentation' for many dishes. For the most complicated constructions – the Gotham seafood salad, tuna tartare and seared tuna – he also provides illustrations, which demonstrate that patience as well as manual dexterity is required. You could also look for a private chef to come to your own kitchen to make the dinner and design the presentations for you. If he is Alan Kehoe, one of his first questions will be whether you have large plates. If not, he will rent them. ∆

On the Waterfront:
Dining Out in Sydney

Sheridan Rogers describes how Sydney's harbour area has been regenerated through the establishment of 'a necklace' of modern restaurants. These not only represent a new approach to design, but also a broader shift away from Anglo-Australian suburban pub culture towards a more Euro-Asian interpretation of central city living.

Sydney is renowned as one of the world's most seductive harbour cities, yet it is only over the past decade that up-market dining venues have appeared around its foreshores. Before Australia's bicentennial year in 1988, the old convict settlement boasted only a few waterside fish-and-chip shops with tables and plastic chairs outside. Seemingly unaware of European traditions since the 17th century, Australian councils previously did not permit restaurateurs to place tables and chairs on public walkways. Archaic liquor licensing laws also discouraged casual dining at indoor-outdoor restaurants, while encouraging rowdy hotel 'garden bars' to serve standard Aussie fare like steaks, chops and sausages. Also, unlike most European cities, Sydneysiders did not live in the city, but in leafy suburbs around it.

Several factors helped to change this regrettable situation. Most importantly, affordable air fares caused an explosion of international travel in the 1980s, which worked two ways for Australia's hospitality industry. First, many more Australians, including restaurateurs and their customers, could more frequently investigate the diverse and urbane outdoor dining habits of Europe and Asia, and would bring back ideas to copy at home. At the same time, many more foreigners – especially the Japanese, Americans and Europeans – began to come to Sydney, with many literally falling in love with its harbour and relaxed, multicultural atmosphere.

In 1988, the bicentennial (a 200-year celebration of the arrival of Captain Cook and the British in Australia) triggered the development of a new waterfront leisure zone called Darling Harbour. Despite protests from local residents, this flashy development on the western side of the city, about a kilometre from Sydney Town Hall, breathed life into a run-down former industrial area and showed Sydneysiders that outdoor dining could be a real bonus, both adding to their enjoyment of the harbour and attracting tourists in droves. The development of inner-city apartments also encouraged people to live in the city, leading to a burst of well-designed little coffee shops, tucked away in interesting available spaces. Around the same time, Rockpool, Sydney's first designer restaurant, came on to the scene. A trio of King's Cross designers called D4 Design (Bill MacMahon, Stephen Roberts and Michael Scott-Mitchell) delivered a seductive and incredibly luxurious fit-out for $1.3 million and put forth the notion, new to Sydney, that a restaurant could seek to become a long-term classic institution. Inspired by Philippe Starck's neo-1930s Art Deco style and updated for the Postmodern period, Rockpool's durable idiosyncratic décor has stood the test of time – as has owner/chef Neil Perry's adventurous Asian-influenced cuisine.

Before the advent of Rockpool, Sydney restaurants had really just been decorated. While good designers like George Freedman and Neville Marsh had made an impact, they didn't kick off a trend. It took a revolution in the Australian food and wine scene during the 1980s for designer fit-outs to really take off. Since then, influential designers have included Burley Katon Halliday (Sailors Thai, The Summit, Box) and McConnell Rayner

Architects (Banc and Wine Banc in Martin Place and the Bathers' Pavilion, Balmoral). Architect and designer Luigi Rosselli also put his European stamp on a number of important restaurants during this period, including the bistro La Mensa in Paddington (1996), the 'theatrical' belmondo in The Rocks (1996) and Pier Function Room at Rose Bay (1997).

Now, at the beginning of the second millennium, there are a number of gleaming white rooms that sit like a necklace around the harbour, stretching from the Harbour Bridge around to Middle Harbour at The Spit. Minimalist in design, they almost disappear to let in the harbour, seducing visitors to partake of the city's hedonistic, bright, breezy lifestyle, and include Catalina and Pier at Rose Bay, the Cruise Bar and Restaurant and the Park Hyatt's harbour kitchen&bar at Circular Quay, Aqua Dining at North Sydney, the Bathers' Pavilion, Watermark and Awaba at Balmoral, Orso and Fresh Ketch at The Spit.

One of the first of these was Awaba café at Balmoral, situated five to six kilometres north of the city on Middle Harbour. Designed by Mark Landini, creative director of Landini Associates, it set a new standard for Sydney cafés when it was refurbished in 1996. 'Responding to its breezy beachside location, we designed Awaba to capture light and views by allowing open-air access to the foreshore and the spectacle of Middle Harbour,' says Landini. Patrons enjoy wall-free dining as concertina aluminium-framed doors fold back along the two beachside facades. A wall-length mirror above the banquettes ensures those who don't face the beach enjoy the same view. Funnily enough, people now take photos of the mirror, mistaking it for the actual view!

A recessed, cast-concrete bar and takeaway servery runs through the restaurant, acting both as a 'funnel' for service staff and a visual barrier to the road and takeaway trade. To enhance views both inside and outside the café, careful manipulation of natural and artificial light was a crucial design consideration. By day, a reflective white gloss-painted ceiling enhances the café's sense of airiness. By night, uplights recessed into the mirrored wall and under the banquettes illuminate the space. The rear lightwall doubles as a giant menu while dividing the restaurant from the kitchen. At night the lightwall acts as an important substitute for the view.

Cruise Bar and Restaurant

Since Awaba, Landini has successfully used mirrors in a number of different venues – the Cruise Restaurant at Circular Quay (2001), Zaaffran in Darling Harbour (1998) and the Botanic Gardens Restaurant & Kiosk in the Botanic Gardens, known as the 'Botanic' (2001): 'I use mirrors to suck in the view, to expand the space and to capture the light. At Awaba, Zaaffran and Cruise Restaurant they reflect the sparkling harbour'.

Landini, former creative director of the Conran Design Group, London, is a fan of the work of British minimalist architect David Chipperfield. His underlying philosophy is to create simple things that last. At the Cruise Bar, a stone's throw from the water's edge at Circular Quay, the sleek, airy interior of the street-level bar takes full advantage of its dress circle positioning with an expansive outdoor promenade at the southern end of the overseas passenger terminal.

White terrazzo floors and walls of white polyurethane and mirrored panelling enhance the light-filled interior – and if that (along with the cocktails) doesn't go straight to your head, the long multicoloured lightwall facing the harbour will; that's if it hasn't turned your complexion green first! Conceived by British visual artist Jeremy Lord, this is the world's largest lightwall (13 metres x 3 metres) with every cell (1.2 metres x 40 centimetres) constantly changing colour as it responds to the sound and movement in the room. Above the

Below
Mark Landini's canny use of mirrors can be seen at his Cruise Restaurant at Circular Quay (2001), where the most is made of a magnificent view of the Opera House.

Cruise Bar is the Cruise restaurant, where Landini has again used mirrors, and on the top level is the sleek, subdued Posh Bar.

Bambu
Just along from the Cruise Bar is Bambu (December 2001), another innovative restaurant-bar addition to the passenger terminal on the Circular Quay foreshore. According to architect and interior designer Misho, one of the stipulations made by the Department of Public Works was that the vista from the street through to the Opera House opposite not be impinged on: 'It was a daunting cold space to work with,' he said, 'so we created a huge sculptural form over the ceiling and along the sidewall to give the feeling of being embraced by an organic form. This allowed me to play around with the light and it also acted as an acoustic baffle.'

The sculpture was constructed using laminated white cardboard panels, an unconventional building material, and is the first of its kind implemented in a commercial situation anywhere in the world. Misho has deliberately kept the interior fit-out subdued in order to provide contrast to the flowing sculpture. Charcoal brown chairs and banquettes, dark polished floorboards and a deep purple-maroon colour scheme on the mezzanine bar level create a warm dining and lounging experience. Former executive chef Xavier Mouche has put together a tantalising menu incorporating dishes from the Mediterranean, Asia, The Land and The Sea. Each one is available as an entrée, encouraging customers to graze their way through the menu.

Cafe Sydney

Not far from the passenger terminal and set well
back from the ferry terminals behind the ugly
Cahill Expressway is the historic Customs House at
the top of which is Cafe Sydney (1999). The interior
design by John Morford (Morford and Associates,
Hong Kong) is stunning and respects the original
architectural features of the room's high ceilings
and huge windows. Inside, the dark timbers, hand-
beaten stainless steel, towering Kentia palms and
enormous artworks of Sydney Harbour marry the
past with the present to create an intimate
sanctuary within the central business district (CBD).

The Colonnade

East of the Customs House and stretching right
up to the entrance of the Opera House is a long
colonnade, along which sit a number of elegant bars
and restaurants. Most of these were completed just
prior to the Sydney 2000 Olympics. They include the ECQ
Bar – a glass box which hovers mid-air over the ferry
terminals; the Quayside Brasserie, Aqualuna Bar and
Restaurant, the Eastbank café/bar/restaurant, Cadmus
and Aria. Suspended between Cadmus and the 10th
floor of the luxurious apartment blocks above the
Colonnade is the Bridge Bar. Perhaps even more than
its unique construction, the Bridge Bar is celebrated
for the extraordinary views – eye-level with the Harbour
Bridge and overlooking the bustle of the harbour,
Circular Quay and the sunset to the west, and the Opera
House, Botanical Gardens and more harbour as far
as the Heads to the east.

Whilst the Colonnade works well spatially, it
terminates rather dismally – and the columns are of

Opposite and above left
The restaurant that shares its concrete podium with the Opera House has recently been refurbished by Dale Jones-Evans and relaunched as Guillaume at Bennelong. Jones-Evans's treatment of the interior has injected a new warmth into the Modernist shell. The space has been relit, the Swan chairs reupholstered and the tables resurfaced with timber. This approach has been reinforced by the inclusion of memorial poles and dreaming paintings, specially commissioned for the scheme.

Above right
Nove Pizzeria at Woolloomooloo identifies more closely with the intimacy of Melbourne restaurants or the European bistro than most of its Sydney counterparts.

questionable design. At the end of the Colonnade is the Opera House, the iconic sculptural building conceived by Danish architect Jørn Utzon in the late 1950s.

Guillaume at Bennelong

Situated on a concrete podium, which juts out over the water, sit three sets of concrete shells, the smallest of which houses the main restaurant, now called Guillaume at Bennelong. The eye-catching shells, clad with small white tiles (some reflective, some matt) reflect, and contribute to, the ever-changing interplay of light, water, ships, ferries and yachts on the harbour.

Due to political opposition, Utzon's original interior designs were scrapped. A number of architects and designers have subsequently worked on the interior of Bennelong, the most recent of whom is Dale Jones-Evans: 'When we took it on, it had the grand gesture of the shell but I felt the space was lacking warmth and intimacy. We wanted to highlight the scale of the existing shell so we spent money relighting it and making the ground plain more intimate', he says. 'We retextured all the furniture and put new fabric on the Swan chairs. And we also resurfaced the tables in timber – previously they were white.'

Jones-Evans employed Barbara Weir, an Aboriginal artist from Utopia (Central Desert, Northern Territory) to paint the large cylinder lights, the small candlelights on the tables and the bar lights in her 'sea-grass dreaming' pattern: 'They throw a warm orange glow which makes the space more intimate', he adds. In the centre are eight Aboriginal memorial poles. Theatrical in design, they hit your eye as soon as you enter. The finance for these was lent by the Opera House Trust, the idea being that it will represent the first significant Aboriginal art collection in the Opera House. It's a big shift away from the sophisticated interior of the previous fit-out, but guaranteed to appeal to tourists. However, there's no bush tucker on the menu. French chef Guillaume Brahimi offers elegant dishes like his signature basil-infused tuna with mustard seed and soy vinaigrette (a small masterpiece) and South Australian blue swimmer crab meat with coriander, avocado and capsicum coulis, and melt-in-your-mouth chargrilled beef tenderloin with Paris mash (rich buttery mashed potatoes *à la Robuchon*) and Merlot sauce.

Further east, around the harbour on the other side of the Botanic Gardens is the Finger Wharf, Woolloomooloo, or 'the Loo' as Sydneysiders affectionately call it, about a kilometre or two from the CBD. It was here at the end of the 19th century that fishermen laid out their catches on the flagged floors of the foreshore and where, during the 20th century, thousands of Australian soldiers boarded ships bound for the Great Wars in Europe and the Middle East.

Above
Originally constructed in 1928
as a Bathers' Pavilion, the
building was established as a
restaurant for 10 years before
it was renovated and
refurbished in 1998 to
become the Bathers' Pavilion.
It is part-owned by Victoria
Alexander, a former
magazine stylist, who
commissioned three different
architects to work on the
building: Alex Popov, Robert
Moore and McConnell Rayner.

Despite efforts by the South Sydney Council to
smarten up the surrounding area, it retains a
rough-and-tumble maritime vitality that takes in
the Australian Navy at one end and the Botanical
Gardens at the other.

In the middle is the Finger Wharf, a
spectacularly long construction built in 1910 by
the Sydney Maritime Trust during a period of
expanding wool, wheat and import trading. The
largest extant timber-pile wharf in the world,
it is a rare surviving example of Federation
architecture applied to a major industrial
structure. Since its refurbishment during the
late 1990s, it has become a fine example of
heritage working with urban development –
fabulous architecturally and an important asset
to the area. It now houses the W Hotel, a huge
interior space that at one time led it to be
nicknamed the 'Cathedral of Commerce', and
a string of private apartments.

Most spectacular is the harbourside
boardwalk or promenade. To stroll along here
on a sunny day is something of an eye-opener,
for this is where sophisticated European
outdoor dining meets Sydney's swanky lifestyle
head-on. There are a number of dining
establishments on the Finger Wharf, not

counting those in the W Hotel, including Otto
Ristorante Italiano, Nove Pizzeria and Pasta Bar,
Manta Ray Seafood Restaurant and Oyster Bar,
Shimbashi Soba Noodle Bar, Kingsley's Steak and
Crab House and a bakery/patisserie and café by
French bakery specialist Laurent Boillon.

Otto

Otto, or 'Spotto' as some social columnists now call
it, is the darling of the group. 'I was invited to look at
this space just over two and a half years ago when
there were still cranes on the wharf,' says the original
owner Maurizio Terzini. 'A lot of restaurateurs
knocked it back. It was a sunny day and I remember
being outside and feeling a sense of tranquillity. It
had everything I wanted – intimate views, calm water,
close to the city. And I liked the fact that
Woolloomooloo was still relatively unexplored.'

Unlike many of the other new restaurants around the
harbour, Otto has more of a European bistro feel, due to
its Melbourne stamp. One of the biggest challenges was
to make the room work in both summer and winter: 'In
winter it becomes small, dark and intimate, rather like
Caffe e Cucina in Melbourne. When we close the doors,
there's a real bistro feel', said Terzini. Dark polished
floorboards, Thonet chairs, crisp white tablecloths and
scattered photos and paintings on the walls give it a

classic bistro look. Wine racks over the bar, cream banquettes along the back wall and a blackboard alongside the open kitchen contribute to this effect. In summer when the doors are flung wide open, the majority of patrons sit outside on pale yellow Philippe Starck plastic chairs: 'I don't like outdoor chairs but these keep the space linear and clean – they're lightweight, plastic and stackable', says Terzini.

'A lot of the atmosphere comes from the people. We offer a European intimacy which people respond to – and I think it proves a restaurant doesn't have to be the most stylish around to be a success. I like my restaurants to be community driven, to suit the local way of life; where the feeling and food are accessible and people can come to eat not dine. Otto's food is not the kind of food my mother would cook, but she would certainly recognise the flavours,' he continues.

Next door at the Nove Pizzeria and Pasta Bar an informal atmosphere reigns. Here, children are welcome. Concrete floors, shiny red and green glass on the stairs leading to the mezzanine, a big communal table inside and bright orange Philippe Starck chairs outside lend a cheerful family atmosphere. Large white bowls of tomatoes and oranges add to the effect.

Bathers' Pavilion

You can take a water taxi from the Finger Wharf, or a ferry from Circular Quay, to Middle Harbour at Balmoral. The taxis pull in beside the charming old-fashioned baths, and as you walk along the boardwalk to the Esplanade, the glass-fronted Watermark Restaurant looks straight at you. An area for outdoor dining has been set aside here and is very popular, whereas at the Bathers' Pavilion (1999), a leisurely walk from Watermark, sadly the Council has not allowed outdoor dining.

Built in 1928 by Mosman Council architect Alfred Hale as a changing shed, it is Spanish Mission in style with Moorish overtones. Having been opened as a restaurant since 1988, a Heritage Order was placed on the building in 1993. After intense opposition from residents to modest development plans for refurbishment, renovation work was completed in the summer of 1999. It now stands gleaming and white with open vistas towards the Heads and over Middle Harbour.

Three firms of architects were commissioned by part-owner Victoria Alexander (Alex Popov, Robert Moore and McConnell Rayner), but it is her stamp on the restaurant that is most apparent. A former advertising and *Vogue* stylist, Alexander has a flair for combining an eclectic array of furniture, fabrics, cloths and napkins including early Australian furniture mixed with modern pieces. The colours and textures are based on a natural palette bringing in the surrounding sea, sky and park, mixed with strong blues and reds as contrast.

Paintings by local artists Kerry Lester, Adrian Lockhart, Graeme Drendel and Jason Benjamin have been used throughout. Popov's cool Scandinavian Zen-Minimalist sensibility and care for the effects of the light and space shine through. Part-owner and chef Serge Dansereau offers up-market dining in the restaurant, and more casual fare is available in the café.

Dining out in Sydney has undergone a dramatic change over the past 15 years. Outdoor dining, especially around the harbour, has become very fashionable and council regulations which once restricted the placement of tables and chairs on pavements have gradually eased, leading to a greater sense of community in the inner city and around the harbour. Sydneysiders have adopted the Italian custom of the *passeggiata* making use of spaces like the Finger Wharf, the Esplanade at Balmoral and the Colonnade to stroll up and down or to drink coffee and gaze at the harbour.

The revolution in the food and wine scene that began in the mid-1980s triggered a design revolution in restaurants, cafés and bars. In many of these venues it is the designer's attention to light, space and view that is most apparent. Davina Jackson, author of *Australian Architecture Now* and former editor of *Architecture Australia*, sees the increase in outdoor dining and the attention to light and views as evidence of Sydney discovering its own spirit of place and relinquishing the tradition of indoor dining inherited from the UK: 'As late as the 1970s, most restaurants were arranged to have intimately enclosed dining rooms, with walls painted in dark colours to heighten the "mood". Today, many Sydney restaurants display the antithesis of "mood". Instead they are often intended to reflect the subtleties of landscape, harbour and weather conditions'.[1]

The open-air dining rooms of Bali and other tropical Asian cities are more recent influences, stimulating the adoption of folding glass doors and window seats with cushions. The focus, once inward, is now outward. Jackson notes that outdoor dining has now become a trend in the suburbs as well. For example: 'The historic city of Parramatta is gradually turning around many of its CBD office buildings to open to the formerly neglected river, with some developers adding new cafés with large outdoor terraces overlooking the water. This gesture will transform the style of the city within the next five years'. ◮

Note
1. Davina Jackson and Chris Johnson, *Australian Architecture Now*, Thames and Hudson (London), 2000. Paperback edn 2002.

Dining Retreats
in Tokyo

The 20-metre-long sushi bar counter at Daidaiya Ginza, designed by Yukio Hashimoto, has glass shelves that display real twigs and artificial roses.

For young Tokyoites, the design of a restaurant requires an entertainment element that is not found in their more traditional domestic lives. **Masaaki Takahashi** charts the recent trends in cuisine and food outlets. He shows, in particular, how a preoccupation with the novel and the innovative has led to designs that have all the theatricality of a film set.

The food service industry seems to have fared well during the recession-stricken Japanese economy of recent times. Although it is currently experiencing a slight setback due to incidents related to BSE (bovine spongiform encephalopathy), annual sales have exceeded two billion yen for the past few years, a figure greater than that of the motor car or steel industry.

With a long cultural tradition, Japan boasts a wealth of local dishes, to which various foreign elements have been added over the last two decades or so. The result is a surprising culinary diversity, especially in larger cities. Chinese and Korean dishes have gained such popularity in Japan that these days they are hardly called 'foreign'.

What is remarkable is the wide range of specialised restaurants in Japan, not only for different types of cuisine they offer but also for the different ways that dishes are prepared and served. These fall into such fine-tuned categories as stir-fries, hotpots, grilled food, sushi, *donburi* ('bowls'), noodles and so on – a variety not found elsewhere, even in New York. This might be attributed to the country's traditional liking for artisanship, which tends to refine things in a narrow domain, and to the efforts of restaurants to distinguish themselves from each other.

Tokyo is flooded with such establishments. Although it is said that the centre of Japanese culinary tradition is the Kansai region, including Osaka and Kyoto, its inhabitants put more emphasis on the dishes themselves than on how they are served, and so restaurant trends are usually born in Tokyo.

The increased popularity of foreign cuisines in Japan is partly due to the many Japanese now travelling abroad thanks to a strong yen. From the 1980s to the 1990s, for example, the country experienced a boom in Thai and other Southeast Asian food, labelled 'ethnic food', followed by a boom in Italian cuisine. The latter was believed by some to be the result of a scheme by a number of trading companies and importers; whatever, it certainly contributed to an enhanced standard of Italian restaurants and shook the status of French cuisine in Japan. Although the boom has now subsided, it represented the beginning of the now common practice, across all types of restaurants, of serving foreign food in a way not adapted to Japanese taste. And in addition, there arose a new trend where real foreign dishes were served in real foreign interiors.

Another origin of design-consciousness in eating and drinking places was the so-called 'café-bar boom' in the 1980s. Café-bars were fashionable drinking establishments, often with simple interiors and monotone colour schemes, typified by bare concrete walls. Open only after five, they served everything that cafés do but with an emphasis on alcoholic drinks. Café-bars became a strong competition to *izakaya*, the more traditional Japanese-style popular pubs. In this arena, a number of interior designers, coordinators and consultants began to call themselves 'space producers'. It was perhaps the

Below left
The Chinese restaurant Niu was designed by Yasumichi Morita. The lamps are modelled on lotus buds.

Below right
A wood panel covers lighting in Niu, which serves more than 60 kinds of Californian wine.

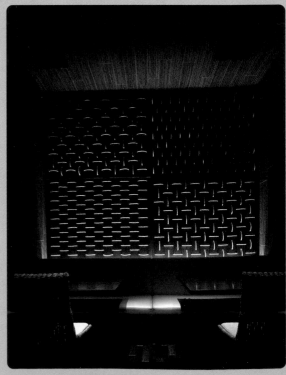

Right
A typical *kissaten* looks closed and can be located almost anywhere.

Below
The Anniversarie (Yasumichi Morita, 2000). Montiors show the 12-hour process of candles burning and melting compressed into 30 minutes. The restaurant is located on the ground floor of a wedding complex, aimed at married couples, or those who plan to marry. The project was designed for special occasions such as anniversaries and memorial days.

period when interior design had the greatest power in attracting customers. Up-market café-bars appealed especially to women, who began to feel more comfortable about drinking, and who by the end of the decade were leading the times. For them, intoxication was not important; they consumed alcohol not to let off steam, as was the case with the hard-working white-collar brigade in the postwar years of rapid economic development, but to better enjoy food – and not vice versa. Comfortable surroundings added to the pleasure, and from that period on trends in Japan's food service industry have centred around women.

In the late 1990s, after the burst of the 'bubble' economy, Japan entered a new era in which trendy restaurants were built and scrapped within about five years. According to Gunshiro Matsumoto, chief editor of the commercial architecture and design magazine *Shotenkenchiku*: 'In the 1970s and 1980s, designers tried to create establishments that lasted. Now they make short-lived ones on low budgets. This may sacrifice quality but it also brings possibilities of innovations out of experiments with new materials and techniques'.

The end of the 1990s saw the culmination of a 'café boom', which still lingers in Harajuku, Aoyama, Daikan'yama and other fashionable towns frequented by the young. The boom was accelerated by mushrooming Starbucks and other foreign-affiliated coffee shops. A number of

Japanese chains responded by introducing cosy, traditional Western-type coffee shops, others by targeting the younger generation with sophisticated interiors – one company was even sued for using a logo and corporate colours too similar to that of Starbucks. The situation could be described as a 'coffee war', with *kissaten* (traditional Japanese coffee and tea houses) the losers. Unlike Western cafés, *kissaten* are more closed than open, with interiors that are plain or home-like, and they serve light meals as well. They probably originated towards the end of the 19th century, and one of the first modern *kissaten* is the Café Paulista, established in 1902 in Ginza, Tokyo.

Typical *kissaten* have spread since the 1930s. In the future, they will survive only in a narrow competitive market, slightly away from the more fashionable trends. The role of cafés, on the other hand, continues to grow. Tokyo cafés welcome the fact that customers now expect to be able to buy meals and alcoholic beverages at their establishments; land prices and rents are high in Tokyo, and serving meals is a simple way to make greater profits. As a result, the café-restaurant-bar trichotomy

is blurred. Ironically this makes me suspect that the pendulum will swing back and the complementary relationship between the three will be revived at the peak of the café's versatility.

Roughly coinciding with the café boom was a resurgence of interest in 'designer restaurants' – those created by famous interior designers. Use of the word 'designer' here is reminiscent of 'designer brands' in the 1980s, when Japanese fashion designers were beginning to acquire international recognition and young people were crazy about buying their clothes. Interior designer Yasumichi Morita says he doesn't like the phrase, but that customers' growing design-consciousness may contribute to raising the overall standard of interior design in restaurants. In addition, the media in Japan is fond of covering topics relating to food and restaurants. A good example was 'Iron Chef', an extremely popular TV show (it was even exported to the US) where chefs played a cooking match. This programme stimulated public interest in cooking and restaurants, and was a catylist for the so-called 'gourmet boom'.

Yoshoku is a Japanised Western cuisine that dates back to the Meiji Restoration in the late 19th century, when the country opened its doors to the West. Now that 'real' Western food has come to stay, the position of *yoshoku* is ambiguous, just like *kissaten* in relation to cafés. 'The Meiji era witnessed drastic changes in people's lives but it was only a hundred years ago. However Westernised they are outside their homes, most Japanese take off their shoes once they come

back home', says Matsumoto, 'so they want something special when eating at a Western-style restaurant. This is why the design of a restaurant should have a sort of entertainment that is not found in everyday lives. Sometimes the design of restaurants seems to have nothing to do with the dishes they serve. But we taste with all our five senses, so I think establishments with much importance attached to design are not necessarily condemned. In fact, no restaurant could lure customers with good dishes alone these days'.

But these remarks might as well be taken with a pinch of salt, because going to a Western-style restaurant is no longer as special for the Japanese as it used to be. In any event, entertaining elements in restaurants come in various forms and scales; for example, some are inspired by Hollywood films or Walt Disney world, and others are entirely original. But do customers really want to patronise a sewer-like restaurant where water runs at regular intervals through huge ducts on the ceiling? Or how about the one where a life-size Chinese doll claps miniature cymbals behind customers when they sit on a toilet seat? These are real examples.

The creature comforts that the Japanese desire when eating out are somewhat different from the expectations of Westerners. According to Yoshiyuki Morii, a renowned interior designer and café-owner: 'Behind the café boom are our housing problems. Cafés are more relaxing than our small houses. So they should not be too special. What café-goers seek is an extension of their own rooms'.

It is true that there appear to be a lot of people who want to 'carry around' their personal space. African, New York and Japanese – Morii's style changes from project to project. His use of real trees and moss in Cube Zen is

Above
A room on the third floor of
Azool (Yoshiyuki Morii, 2000).
Red paper lamp shades
and the use of a zebra
pattern target couples.

Right, top
The carpet room on the third
floor of Azool. Allowing people
to remove their shoes in bars
has become a popular way
of encouraging customers
to relax.

Right, bottom
A room on the third half-floor
of Azool. The animal-print
fabric conjures up the kitsch
mood of a hotel.

Opposite
A room in Azool showing
the intimate interior.

in the spotlight. Azool, another famous work in Nishiazabu, is divided into several secluded rooms with low ceilings and dim lighting, each with a different interior design; for example one has a leopard-print sofa, another a carpet where you take off your shoes. These intimate rooms are intended to bring people closer to each other – a theme behind all of Morii's work. 'The Japanese are shy,' he comments, 'so the design of restaurants and cafés needs to be the kind that makes communication with each other easier. This is why, for example, I created a curved counter. It prevents people from facing others directly. Places for eating and drinking are indispensable backdrops of the social lives of us shy people. I would say we might expect more of restaurants' and bars' interior design than Westerners.' Nishiazabu used to be quite ordinary, but with the introduction of restaurants and clubs by famous designers it has now become one of Tokyo's most fashionable areas.

So far, there has been no city planning in Tokyo, not even after the massive destruction of the Second World War. The city has sprawled like an octopus spreading its tentacles, and the government, as well as its citizens, takes little care to preserve the landscape. Apart from the right of light, there are virtually no legal restrictions on what can be built where, and the result is a mixture of buildings of diverse styles and designs, especially in town. For example, below a modern skyscraper by Kenzo Tange we see a group of shabby wooden apartment houses. Interior designer Yukio Hashimoto's opinion is that this chaos will be rectified sooner or later and that there is no need for restrictions on the landscape. 'Chaos has merit as well,' he adds, 'because it is important to experiment with various designs. From these experiments, design-conscious younger generations and their new cultures are now emerging in several fields. They are ready to accept and appreciate innovations such as the recent Japanese-style *nouvelle cuisine*. Japan has caught up with the West in food and clothing. And only recently have we begun to care about shelter. Our increasing interest in restaurants and bars is a sign.'

It is not certain how long it will take before the good is sifted from the bad, but it is true that the attitudes of Tokyoites towards architectural and interior design are changing. Many young people who used to prefer *izakaya* are now going to sophisticated places and paying more than double the price. The Japanese younger generations are setting new standards. But I fear that their innovativeness could mean the loss of our cultural traditions when I see, for example, that they are beginning to take a dislike to ordinary Japanese recipes. The eye and palate of future generations depend on how seriously designers and chefs of the present generation think about their creations. We need to be aware that architecture can have a greater influence on us than architects and designers imagine. It is architecture as well as food that makes people.

This restaurant, which opened in May 2000, is the seventh and largest of the Daidaiya chain. Ginza is one of Tokyo's most prestigious neighbourhoods, with its many classy brand shops, and is often a destination for tourists from abroad. However, the restaurant is located closer to Shinbashi, a typical business quarter, than to Ginza. It is on the first floor of a commercial building, Ginza Nine, under an elevated highway, with the entrance on the ground floor. This restaurant-bar accommodates 370, and the floor is 997 square metres, of which the kitchen occupies 120 square metres.

The approach is decorated with pinhole-sized specks of light scattered over a black surface, just like twinkling stars or fireflies. Inside, the entrance foyer uses Oya-ishi stone (a kind of volcanic tuff), which makes customers feel relaxed. In the middle of the floor is a 60-metre-long hall extending straight to the back; a variety of Japanese-style rooms appear one after another as you walk along it. The first is a cigar and bar lounge, the second a tatami room next to two cones, reminiscent of the white pebble garden of Ginkakuji Temple (one of the waiters calls the cones Mount Fujis). Next, at the heart of the restaurant, is a space like a Noh stage. Still further back are a 20-metre-long sushi counter on the left and a private area on the right, partitioned by red hemp screens like mosquito nets.

Designer Yukio Hashimoto says he paid homage to Japanese art by creating a collage of elements from temples, Shinto shrines, Japanese gardens and tea-ceremony rooms. The idea behind the minimal Japanese-style space is the East viewed from the West, or the typical Japanese-style Westernised space – a recent design trend. On a trip to Kyoto, Hashimoto was inspired by the design and aura of the shrine on Kuramayama, a holy mountain. The interior of the restaurant in a sense represents a journey like his, from Tokyo to Kyoto and back.

Each area in the restaurant is illuminated by a different kind of lamp: balls of light slowly wave above the hall, and raised tatami-matted areas have lights embedded in the floor, gracefully illuminating a cylinder of lace that reaches the ceiling. Above the table here are three moderately dimmed small pinhole lamps providing exquisite indirect lighting. The other tatami-matted zone in the room has a shimmering wall of handmade *washi* (Japanese paper) with a light within. And from the ceiling of the sushi counter area, countless pendant lamps hang like wind bells; though only tiny five-watt thumb-sized bulbs, gently blinking in groups, the number is overwhelming. The red partitions in the private zone are translucent, but good lighting gives the place a mysterious atmosphere almost like an opium den.

The Daidaiya Ginza is currently rated as one of the best *iyashi-kei* restaurants. *Iyashi-kei* is a buzzword of contemporary Japanese pop culture meaning 'healing'. Many people seek *iyashi-kei* in their lives overstressed by recession and other hardships; customers are mainly businesspeople from offices in the vicinity, though there are also a lot of couples and female groups. Dishes are Japanese-style *nouvelle cuisine* alongside traditional dishes such as sushi. Ingredients usually flavoured only with soy sauce are treated with unexpected seasonings and spices, and are aesthetically arranged on the plates – bream seasoned with grated Japanese radish and sour orange juice, or flatfish with lightly roasted *karasumi* (the ovaries of mullet in salt). Some dishes are fusions of Japanese and Western cuisines, some resemble Californian fare; others are just hard to imagine from the menu description.

The client wanted to reproduce the atmosphere of Tawaraya, a small, prestigious Japanese-style inn in Kyoto renowned for its good service, which is also believed to accept only those with a letter of introduction. An average customer at Daidaiya Ginza pays more than 50 dollars, and the restaurant hopes to achieve a monthly turnover of 100 million yen.

Above
The restaurant is on the first floor of a building under a highway. The entrance is below a red panel.

Right
Central area of Daidaiya Ginza. A counter surrounds two pebble cones which a waiter calls two Mount Fujis.

Around Shinjuku station, neon lights are flashing while comedians on a giant TV screen attempt to entertain the 3.3 million passengers who pass through the station daily. Along with noisy commercials from loudspeakers and incessant flows of pedestrians, this makes the area look just like a scene from *Blade Runner* – especially when people open their umbrellas in the rain. With all the things a city can have, from fashionable restaurants to *soba* (buckwheat) noodle stands and even a red light district, Shinjuku represents all of Tokyo.

Ken's Deli and Cafe and Ken's Dining Shinjuku, which opened in October 1999, are situated on the ground floor and basement, respectively, of a building in one of the town's most crowded areas. This location led designer Yasumichi Morita to create a simple facade with no overdesigned flashy details. Makeshift panels for use in construction sites are utilised for the entrance.

The major part of the ground floor is occupied by a showcase-like freezer, and the mirrors on the counter facing the wall are lined with rows of small lamps, somewhat reminiscent of a beauty parlour. The walls of the stairs to the basement are covered with tatami (rush mats). Tatami are usually used for the floor of a Japanese-style room, so using them in this way is fresh for the Japanese. The basement's floor (355 square metres) is a trapezoid that gets narrower towards the back. In the centre is a large granite table (6 x 4.2 metres) with two large shaded lamps on it. The seating includes three sofas for couples in a dim corner of the otherwise well-lit restaurant. The walls are covered with a layer of panels with Chinese rubbings attached to them, and the ceiling is composed of a clear mirror and a wooden lattice above it.

The lights are Morita's original designs. Especially unusual are the pole-shaped lights at the sofas. These consist of acrylic pipes 100 millimetres across with a sheet of resin-treated *washi* (Japanese paper) calligraphy work inside. The restaurant seats 110 in all.

Customers are mostly female and in their early twenties. Like many other restaurants in Tokyo, the chic interior would look more becoming if there were a greater proportion of older customers, perhaps thirty-somethings. Slim boys and girls in the latest fashions look somewhat overwhelmed by the atmosphere. The situation here is representative of the rest of Tokyo: stylish establishments target only the younger generations.

The interior is present-day Art Deco with a hint of Chinese, a combination of shiny metallic materials and dark wood – cool and beautiful. The interior and particularly the ceiling are reminiscent of the American Bar by Adolf Loos. The mirrors and the huge mass of granite give a sort of coldness to the space; however, this might be interpreted as spice by the young. For these trend-conscious Tokyo diners, both the quality of the food and the quality of the interior have to be hip.

The restaurant is operated by Chanto Food Service. President Ken'ichiro Okada is charismatic in the Japanese food service industry. A chef himself, he owns a chain of more than 30 restaurants nationwide, with gross annual sales of seven billion yen. Before opening this particular deli and restaurant he carried out his research in New York, and came back with the idea of adding sushi and *onigiri* (rice balls) to the deli's menu. The restaurant features Okada's much-acclaimed Japanese-style *nouvelle cuisine*, a rare mix of Japanese and Western dishes like fresh foie gras steak with risotto flavoured with white miso.

Yasumichi Morita has created interiors that are just right for Okada's culinary concepts. In the early days, for example, he hung numerous woks all over a red wall, making an instant leap to prominence in the industry. He favours the frequent use of mirrors, modern adaptations of Chinese landscape paintings, vases and other ancient handiwork, German avant-garde designer Ingo Maurer's lamps and bold graphic work, all contributing to establishing the impressive style of Ken's restaurants.

Above
The entrace is set back and bare construction panels make the signage. Scratches look like a *kanji* message.

Right
The ground-floor eating space. The right wall, decorated with shaded lamps, displays monochrome photos of Japanese foods.

Daikan'yama is a neighbourhood popular among fashionable young people, and boasts a multitude of trendy shops and boutiques. Near Daikan'yama station, the wine restaurant Le Cocon, opened in October 2000, occupies the ground floor and basement of a building which used to be an apparel manufacturer's showroom and office connected by a stairwell. The neighbourhood is rather quiet as it is back from a main street.

The restaurant's designer, Hideo Horikawa, is also its owner, and he can often be seen serving customers. Horikawa calls himself the world's first architect ever with qualifications for a sommelier. It is his rule to be the owner of the establishments he designs because he wants to do just what he wants. With such avant-garde architecture as houses pierced with beams, Horikawa might not belong to the mainstream of Japanese architectural design. However, Le Cocon received the Yohji Yamamoto Prize in 2001 from the Japanese Society of Commercial Space Designers, an indicator that his style is beginning to be recognised more widely and will serve as a good stimulus to the industry.

Opening the entrance door with its inlaid cracked wood at the centre, there is a slightly irregular-shaped counter on the right – a piece of natural wood with small cracks. On the left are decorations based on the wall of a cave, covering the best part of the wall and the ceiling and extending to the roof of the stairwell at the back. These are made up of 4624 three-millimetre-thick triangular plywood pieces, and lamps scattered here and there emphasise the three-dimensional nature of the uneven geometric surface. Seen alone, this structure is reminiscent of Coop Himmelblau and also looks like Kurt Schwitters' Merzbau refined by rhythm. But the design of the basement is completely different, and as a whole the restaurant is truly original.

At the end of a long passage on the ground floor is the stairwell leading down to the main dining area in the basement. One would normally expect tables and chairs here, but instead the seats are all Japanese-style – a cushion on a cypress floor. This is a very relaxing way of sitting for the Japanese, and also makes the ceiling look higher, an effect that the architect must have calculated. One part of the wall sticks out to form a huge grey cocoon containing a row of nine smaller cocoons of varying sizes. These are private rooms accommodating up to twelve or so people, and seats here are also Japanese-style. Coming through an extremely narrow passageway and seeing an orderly row of cocoons, one has the strange feeling of straying into a gigantic underground nest for insects, or a primitive village of clay houses. The cocoons are covered with stucco, and in places gravel has been fancifully scraped off the surface. They are earth colours and at night the lights are dimmed, and gentleness and calm prevail. During the day the mysterious atmosphere is somewhat reduced by sunlight.

Filippa Giordano's version of a Puccini aria impressively fills the air, amplified by an artistic valve-type audio set assembled by an expert. Dishes are French-based, and the emphasis is on serving good wines which are not too expensive. The age group of customers varies; some work in boutiques and other fashion-related establishments in the neighbourhood. If the whole project is compared to a cocoon, they are the larvae inside, separated from the real world. This design type has recently become popular as many Tokyo restaurant-goers demonstrate a need for closed, dark shelters to escape from reality.

Horikawa's fondness for secluded space has led him to create restaurants resembling caves or a rabbit's nest made of countless twigs. Of special mention is Mayu ('cocoons'), which has cocoon-like private rooms made of *washi*. This restaurant is said to have triggered the recent boom in private rooms in Tokyo restaurants; in fact, it has become so popular that a second is scheduled to be opened in Ginza.

It is Horikawa's belief that surprising gimmicks are necessary in a place for eating and drinking. ⚼

Right
The ground floor. A cracked wooden table with ceiling and walls decorated with panels based on a computer graphic of a cave. Stairs at the back lead to the basement.

Far right
Small rooms like these are trendy in Tokyo.

Museum (Quality) Dining

Stephan Marc Klein explores the increasing importance of dining in a museum context. As restaurants have become integral to the museum experience, they have also become a defining part of an institution's identity. Whereas the Café Sabarsky at the Neue Galerie in New York evokes Secessionist period Vienna, the curators of the Asia Society, in the same city, have consciously chosen to use the modern space in the Garden Court Café to exhibit works by contemporary Asian and Asian-American artists.

Museums, by definition, are about definition. Museums define what societies value, what they preserve and what they discard. In short, museums define taste.[1] Entering a museum is akin to entering a temple, or a Japanese tea house. The messy, noisy, quotidian outside world disappears, replaced by a world of idealised and integrated aesthetic harmony. Within, we adjust our behaviour to suit this world, and we adjust our expectations. We expect beauty, certainty, truth. Describing an object as 'museum quality' cloaks it in an aura, and the museum aura can affect all aspects of the museum experience.[2]

The purpose of museum visiting has traditionally been considered either aesthetic or educational, its success measured by what the visitor retains from the visit. Visitor research has shown, however, that the success of exhibitions has as much to do with whether visitors have meaningful experiences – whether they have found meaning in what they have encountered, whether they have been in some way transformed by their experience in the museum – as it does with what they remember of the exhibit. Exhibition developer Barry Lord has written: 'It is important to notice that this apprehension of meaning, like all transformation, is primarily an affective experience rather than a cognitive one. Museum exhibitions address our awareness of the world, and affect our attitudes and values, all of which are much more fundamental than our knowledge of specific facts about the subject matters'.[3]

Since museums are so involved with issues of taste, an integral component of 'attitudes and values', it is ironic that of all the sense modalities, museum exhibitions least engage the sense of taste. Few exhibits include displayed objects that can be touched, much less eaten. Nevertheless, eating in museums has a long history. Furthermore, from the institution of the first museum dining with the installation of a refreshment room at the South Kensington (now Victoria and Albert) Museum in London, when it opened in 1857, museums through design and menu have often capitalised on the museum aura and sought to extend it into the restaurant.

When director Henry Cole decided, in the 1860s, to expand the refreshment rooms in the South Kensington Museum, he hired the firm of William Morris, which included Philip Webb, Burne-Jones and the painter Edward Poynter, to decorate them because he wanted the rooms to be works of art, fitting with his idea that the museum buildings be used as a 'living' exhibit. The rooms still live, with aura still intact, as exhibition rooms for decorative art. Occasionally they are also still used for dining. In order to increase revenues, the Victoria and Albert, like many museums these days, rents its exhibition spaces for private functions. Ironically, the refreshment rooms originally intended to broaden the public that would visit the museum are now only available for dining by those corporations and individuals (including their guests) who can afford to rent out the rooms. For those who can afford the hefty rental fees, the aura of the rooms, enhanced by their history, makes them attractive venues for private events.[4]

Design and Narrative

I am in the Café Sabarsky at the recently opened Neue Galerie in New York City, a museum devoted to early 20th-century German and Austrian art and design. Neue Galerie, designed by architect Anabelle Selldorf, occupies an eclectic Fifth Avenue mansion, originally designed in 1914 by Carrére and Hastings for industrialist William Starr Miller. The café, in the mansion's former ground-floor library, has retained the room's *fin-de-siècle* general décor of dark wood panelling. The additions necessary for transforming the room into a restaurant are in the same Vienna Secession style as many of the objects displayed in the galleries upstairs and designed by some of the same designers and artists represented in the museum. Josef Hoffmann designed the crystal lighting fixtures, Adolf Loos the furniture and Otto Wagner the banquette upholstery.

A bentwood newspaper rack, typical of Viennese cafés, stands by the door, a bentwood coat hanger by the display of tortes and other desserts. A chrome and glass display refrigerator, also typical of Viennese cafés, dominates the far end of the room. Viennese-style waltzes play softly over the speaker system, providing an aural backdrop to the murmur of conversation and clinking tableware. It is a late-winter afternoon, dark already. The street-lamps and car lights glimmering through the blackness outside could as well be coming from some Mittel-European city's *strasse*. I order a *wiener wurst mit kartoffelsalat*; my companion Anna an *ungarisches rindsgulasch mit spætzle*.

After dining, we tour the museum, feeling a glow from what has seemed to us a wonderfully accurate rendition of superb Viennese food, and from the general *gemutlicht* atmosphere of the museum, a salubrious environment for viewing the Schieles, Klimts, Beckmanns, work of the Bauhaus, the Vienna Secession and others. We feel as if we've spent the afternoon in Vienna.

Café Sabarsky takes advantage of the aura that infuses the objects museums display. Our dining experience 'tuned' us for our encounters with the exhibits, framing our mood and transporting us into one of the places and times in which the art and design were produced. Conversely, the food and dining experience was authenticated and enhanced by being part of the museum. Scott Gutterman, deputy director of the museum, points out that this was intentional: 'Café Sabarsky is an integral part of the Neue Galerie. Historically it refers to the great Viennese cafés that were centres of intellectual and artistic life. Aesthetically, it is an extension of the work that is shown in the galleries. Last but not least, it serves the best coffee in New York'.

Museums, like other institutions, employ design as one of many instruments for creating narratives about who they are and what they do, and which produce what we accept as the 'real', 'natural' or 'true' version of the past and the present, even though the hegemony of these versions might have been contested behind the scenes or outside the museum's walls. Using a middle-class Viennese café to metonymically represent both Germany and Austria doesn't just enhance the museum visit; it sets the visit within a mythologised, comfortable context. It creates a narrative, aided by its design, which immerses visitors in a romanticised version of the period while eliding economic and political upheaval, poverty, malaise, and the resultant rising tide of fascism and anti-Semitism that were also dominant characteristics of the period.

The Neue Galerie with its café, it seemed, was in part a project to rehabilitate or put a positive spin on pre-Second World War Germany and Austria and claim their centrality to European culture. Visitors moving through the entrance section of the permanent exhibition at the Holocaust Memorial Museum in Washington DC experience a very different narrative of Germany and Austria before the war.

The recently opened Garden Court Café at the Asia Society in New York City, designed by Voorsanger and Associates, offers a dining experience similar to that at the Café Sabarsky, complementing and enhancing the museum viewing experience while itself being enhanced by its museum setting. Likewise, it too conveys a narrative that has an agenda for its politics of culture. Like the Café Sabarsky, it portrays only positive aspects of the cultures represented by the museum. However, the Asia Society design – including its café – also attempts to critique, and present an alternative to, a Western-centric viewpoint that exoticises, primitivises and essentialises the cultures of Asia.

This restaurant was part of a major renovation of the building, originally designed in 1980 by Edward Larabee

Barnes, that included renovation of all the galleries and the addition of a skylit lobby and grand entrance stair. Unlike the Café Sabarsky, the Garden Court Café does not attempt to literally re-create the context of the geographic areas and time periods represented in the museum's collections and displays, nor is it clothed in a traditional oriental style. The design of the renovation, like the original building, is Modernist, and uses industrialised materials such as a skylight roof of steel and glass. Artworks by contemporary Asian and Asian-American artists punctuate the café and public circulation spaces, all connoting that Asia is not just the antiques displayed in the museum's galleries but also a part of the contemporary world. The design employs subtle strategies to evoke the ambience of an Asian garden. Tables are spaced far apart among trees, all of species native to Asia. At one end, a large contemporary sculpture by Chinese artist Xu Guadong emulates the kind of natural rock that might be found in a traditional Chinese garden. Another contemporary sculpture by Indonesian artist Heri Dono hangs from the skylit roof. Many

Right and below
The Tower Restaurant for the Museum of Scotland, Edinburgh (Benson + Forsyth Architects, 1998). Set apart from the museum exhibits in a penthouse, it looks out over the rooftops of Edinburgh, linking the city to the museum exhibition which traces the history of Scotland.

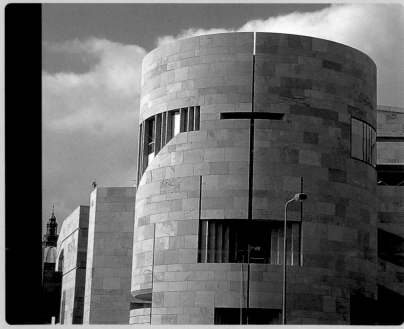

of the surfaces are veneered with light-coloured wood. The menu is Pan-Asiatic.

When I lunched there (on a quite fine pulled duck and green onion dumplings in a cucumber timbale with blood orange vinaigrette), new-age Asian-style music was playing softly over the speaker system. After lunch, viewing sculptures of Buddhas, Bodhisattvas and Hindu gods and goddesses from the museum's collection of traditional Asian art, I had the feeling that my mood – peaceful and serene – was, if not created then perhaps enhanced by my experience in the Garden Court Café.

Vishakha N Desai, Director of the Museum and Cultural Programs, affirms that both food and form follow function in the café and museum: 'The nouvelle pan-Asian cuisine offered in the Garden Court Café along with the innovative music playing in the background offer the visitor not just a complete culinary and aesthetic experience but also an exciting sense of contemporary Asia. The modern design of the interior that uses materials often associated with Asia in new ways, and the interactive technology using new media in the lobby, are part of a conscious effort to portray Asia as very much in step with the rhythms of globalisation and modernity. We're trying to dispel a frequently held misperception of Asia or Asian cultures as something static, strictly traditional and mired in the past ... Collectively, it all adds up to a celebration of Asia's diversity and vitality that we hope our visitors will not only learn from but share in'.

Both the Neue Galerie and the Asia Society use similar strategies in putting their dining facilities, via design and menu, to use in changing the perceptions of visitors about the societies their museums represent. However, due to the relationship of the museums to contemporary societal as well as historical issues beyond their walls, the politics of each differs: one creates myth while the other demythifies.[5]

Museum Dining and the Museum Mission Statement
When designers and architects are sensitive to the narrativising potential of museum restaurants and cafés, they can create places for eating that support and augment the museum's mission statement, and not simply design an aesthetic 'museum-quality' atmosphere for dining.

The Tower Restaurant in the Museum of Scotland in Edinburgh, designed by Benson + Forsyth Architects and opened in 1998, uses locations as well as design to support the museum's mission statement. The roof-garden restaurant on the museum's top floor is entered through the restaurant's own lobby and elevator as well as through the museum. Development manager Mark Rowley, who designed its interior, says: 'There is something of a museum quality about the space, with the furnishings looking a little like well-used exhibits in the museum – more so at night when each table is pin-spotted. Comfort and luxury were paramount ... There was a conscious effort to discourage "tea and cake" business in the early stages as this would have diluted the restaurant concept – which was difficult enough to project as most assume a museum restaurant is essentially a tearoom or café'.

The restaurant, which advertises itself as one of the city's finest dining experiences, is open for lunch and also in the evenings when the museum is closed. While modern in style, the museum and restaurant use some local materials; for example, Clashach stone in the museum and Aberdeen Angus beef in the restaurant. The cylindrical turret entrance of the museum is in part derived from such medieval Scottish castles as Dunstaffnage. The Tower Restaurant was a part of the original museum design, unlike many museum restaurants such as the Court Restaurant in the British Museum in London, designed by Norman Foster, which have either been installed long after the museum was built, or have changed their original design through renovation.

The Scottish museum, contrary to the practice of most museums where the exhibition design is independent and after the fact of the architecture, takes the approach of integrating interior and exterior architecture with the exhibits, which chronologically narrate and celebrate the history of Scotland. As the museum is set in the centre of Scotland's capital, a city with a long history expressed through its varied architecture, part of the architects' charge was to design a museum in which the building not only exhibited objects on its walls and in its cases but also exhibited the city beyond the museum's walls. Architect Gordon Benson has described this as giving visitors 'physical postcards, as it were, of Edinburgh ... These glimpses of the outside impinging on the inside will complete the whole show'.[6]

In contrast to the British Museum where the restaurant, at the end of two symmetrical, monumental flights of stairs, sits atop and overlooks its central court, roofed by Foster's great skylit lamella arches, the Tower Restaurant turns its back to the museum interior and its grand central hall. Set apart in a penthouse, it instead looks out over the rooftops and spires of Edinburgh, focusing directly on the castle, the heart of Edinburgh and its most enduring symbol. Thus, paradoxically, the Tower Restaurant provides a visual break from the museum visiting experience while it visually links the museum to its city.

Today's museum restaurants and cafés are a legacy of earlier cafeterias and lunchrooms which were included in the museums of the Progressive Era when boards of directors and administrators began to realise the museum's potential as an instrument of moral education and reform for the masses.

Museums and Consumption

Today's museum restaurants and cafés are a legacy of earlier cafeterias and lunchrooms which were included in the museums of the Progressive Era (1860s through to the 1920s) when boards of directors and administrators began to realise the museum's potential as an instrument of moral education and reform for the masses. Museum lunchrooms made museums more appealing to more people, including new groups of museum-goers such as women and the working classes, and also encouraged people to stay longer.

These days, ironically, the same economic forces that are pushing museums to reach out to increase their audiences are encouraging the proliferation of exclusively priced museum-based dining facilities – both destination dining and those requiring the purchase of museum entrance tickets – and have, as in the example mentioned earlier at the Victoria and Albert Museum, resulted in museums renting out their exhibition spaces for private functions. Museums are thus becoming more populist as more people visit them, yet more elitist as only more affluent patrons can afford their amenities.

Museums are also becoming more overtly concerned with consumption. For example, it is possible to view the many 'blockbuster' special exhibitions of recent years in art museums that have drawn such large crowds as manufacturing a longing to consume (acquire) the objects displayed. These longings are then slaked at the inevitable gift shops that form the gauntlets visitors must run to exit the exhibitions. Perhaps when the next stage of the museum visit is the refreshment break in the upscale dining facility, eating and drinking affords a sublimated consumption of high culture, satisfying the 'appetite' worked up through encounter with the exhibited objects. In doing so, museum restaurants support the most-often unarticulated, yet essential, aspects of museums' missions – to be financially remunerative and to provide touchstones for visitors' status-conscious self-definitions.

Restaurants and Exhibitions: Extending the Possibilities

Whether in central reception atria or on rooftop terraces, most museum restaurants are separated from exhibitions. This is in part due to concern for the preservation of fragile objects on display, and also due to the conviction that the dining experience should constitute a break from exhibition viewing. However, beginning with the Morris refreshment rooms mentioned earlier, museum dining rooms have also been integrated with exhibition viewing.

architects, is undergoing a major renovation, designed by DMCD Design – significantly, exhibition designers. The new restaurant will have flat-screen monitors suspended on wires above the tables showing a variety of videos, including montages of the exhibitions inside the museum and longer, didactic tapes about subjects related to museum exhibits. A central visual feature of the restaurant will be a changing 'banner' with the names of the currently 400-plus men and women who have been in space. The new restaurant will thus become tied to the museum's celebratory narrative of America's achievements in air and space.

In the aptly named Newsbyte Café in the Newseum in Arlington, Virginia, designed by exhibition designer Ralph Appelbaum, diners can, using computer terminals at the eating counters, access web sites around the world that report on the news. The café has

The exhibitions, functioning as décor, extend the museum aura powerfully into the dining spaces. Eating in such spaces perhaps creates a 'taste' for an aesthetic style of life. For example, the Petrie Court Café, a coffee and snack bar on the ground floor of the Metropolitan Museum of Art in New York City, not only looks out via a glass wall at Central Park but is set in the museum's European Sculpture and Decorative Arts gallery. Diners sit under the blank yet watchful eyes of large bronze and stone figurative sculptures by Auguste Rodin, Aristide Maillol and Charles Despiau. The museum's main restaurant, slated for renovation, will also integrate with exhibits such as the future Roman Sculpture Garden.

Restaurants in museums can become part of the educational and experiential aspects of the museum visit. The Washington DC National Air and Space Museum restaurant, originally designed by Helmuth, Obata and Kassabaum

two menus – one for the refreshments offered and another, the 'Web Menu', for the web sites that can be accessed. The museum also displays objects from its collection in cases hung on the walls of the café'.

All restaurants are much more than culinary experiences; they are a form of participatory theatre, 'an elaborate performance of gender, social class and self-identity'.[7] Because eating is so basically sensual and nonrational at its root, it is a powerful trigger of feelings and memories. When we go to a French restaurant, for example, we expect at some inchoate level to suspend our disbelief and be transported to France. The narrative of France that we participate in through eating in a French restaurant is a simplified and romanticised one, often set in the past, that presents an essentialised France – charming, conflict-free and timeless.

The restaurants in restoration museums and at heritage sites, such as the Bullard Tavern in the late 18th- to early 19th-century village restoration in Sturbridge, Massachusetts, are striking examples of

Notes
1. The flip side of taste-making is that museums, through the creation of taste-canons, define us as well as the objects they contain. Through visiting museums we define who we are and our place in the social order; we are the ones with good taste (with all the privileges and power granted thereby).
2. Capitalising on the aura museums can convey to their restaurants. A recent review of dining in New York museums is 'The fine art of dining', *Museums New York: Special Edition*, Winter, 2002, pp 20–21.
3. B Lord, 'The purpose of museum exhibitions', in B and GD Lord (eds) *The Manual of Museum Exhibitions*, Altamira Press (Walnut Creek, Cal), 2002, p 17.
4. In this article I use the notion of museum aura to examine

the participatory theatre of dining out. Not only are these restaurants usually designed in the period style of the restoration, often occupying restored buildings such as taverns and inns, they also frequently feature dishes of the period, have waiting-staff dressed in period costume and provide entertainment typical of the period, all in service of extending to the dining experience the museum's mission to give visitors a taste of a historical era.

However, the museum could go further in using the restaurant and related exhibits to expose the social and political complexities of the period. Diners experience this historical era as one of abundance and one in which a classless society existed. The slaves and indentured servants necessary to produce the

experience of life during the period. And adding eating to the Lower East Side Tenement Museum, which occupies an actual tenement in New York City, could enrich visitors' experiences with the smells of cooking that permeated the building in the early 20th century and convey in a visceral and experiential way the importance of eating, both as social ritual in terms of connecting immigrant families with their pasts, and as economic exigency in terms of conveying the limited range of choices available to the lower classes.

Whether matzo at a Jewish Seder or communion wafers in a Catholic Mass, eating is about ingesting symbolic meanings as well as sustenance. For example, when we eat foods selected from the booths of regional American cuisines in the Smithsonian Museum of American History in Washington DC, we 'consume' America and bond with it. The adage 'we are

how, via design, it can enhance the experience of eating in museums, and conversely how, by supporting the museum's mission statement, eating in museum restaurants can enhance visitors' experiences of the exhibitions. I focus primarily on restaurants that attempt to appeal to diners by providing quality cuisine and décor, as opposed to the traditional museum cafeteria or brown-bag lunch room so often tucked away in dark basement corners.
5. According to Roland Barthes: 'Myth is depoliticized speech'. R Barthes, *Mythologies*, Hill and Wang (New York), 1972, p 142.
6. Reported in C Mckean, *The Making of the Museum of Scotland*, National Museum of Scotland Publishing (Edinburgh), 2000, p 76.
7. J Finkelstein, 'Dining out: the hyperreality of appetite', in R Scapp and B Seitz (eds) *Eating Culture*, State University of New York Press (Albany), 1998, p 203.
8. b hooks, 'Eating the other: desire and resistance', in Scapp and Seitz op cit, p 181.

actual meals in the period represented have vanished, along with any awareness of the long hours of repeated backbreaking labour that bound women to their homes and kitchens.

Great and mostly untapped potential exists for museums such as history and science centres to employ the notion of dining as participatory theatre in their exhibitions. Adding typical military mess-hall food or even C or K rations to the more usual food offered in the café, and designing the café itself to resemble an army mess-hall, could enhance the experience of the Second World War at military museums such as the D-Day Museum in New Orleans or the Imperial War Museum in London. Eating the food of late 18th-century America in a restaurant resembling a tavern of the time in connection with the current 'Life after the Revolution' exhibition at the Smithsonian American History Museum in Washington DC, could give visitors both a figurative and literal 'in the gut'

what we eat' can be interpreted to have meaning in symbolic social and psychological, as well as physical, terms. Via everything experienced within them, museums are for ever telling stories. Their narratives intertwine, they nest within one another, modify each other and create at metalevels new metanarratives. Museum dining is part of these continual, complex narrativising processes. If in its restaurant a natural history museum includes cuisines from the cultures represented in its exhibition halls, what will this tell us about these cultures?

Can dining in museums serve a new mission for museums of demythifying the world, or will it serve processes of mythification? Will the participatory theatre of eating 'exotic' cuisine lead to a 'commodification of otherness', as bell hooks has written?[8] Or can the act of eating, in conjunction with learning about the relationship of the product we are consuming to the economic, political, social and technical processes that produced it, lead us to some understanding of how the other half lives? ⚐

Menu-Driven Design:
An Interview with James Soane of
Project Orange

For architect James Soane, the relationship between food and design in a restaurant is integral. In a conversation with **Helen Castle** he explains how over the years he has devised his own distinctive 'thematic' approach – a process that is not only accessible to clients but also gives full consideration to the menu and the particular cuisine that is served.

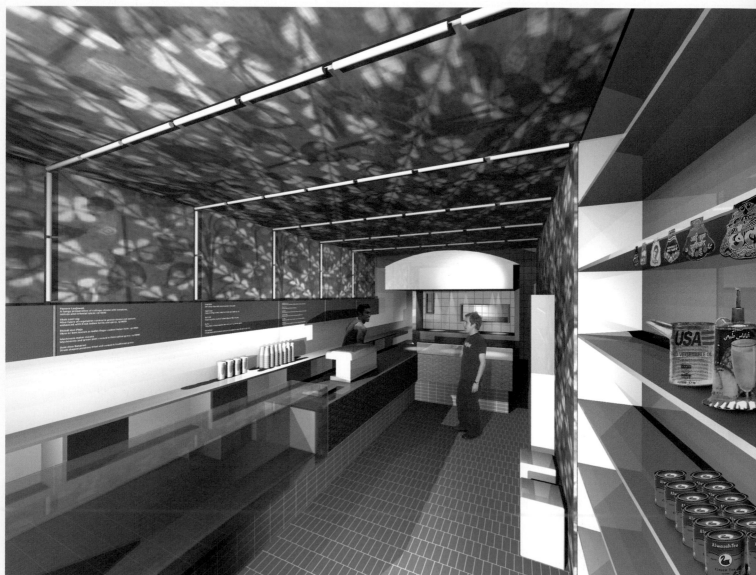

It is clear from talking to James Soane that more than anything else he and his partner Christopher Ash are intent on creating the right setting for each client. For Soane, every project has to 'stand on its own'. This amounts to a rejection of signature architecture and its accompanying autographed vocabulary, which is rolled out in every instance with 'a suitcase of details'. If there is a consistent formal approach, it surfaces in 'an overall sense of trying to express the condition of the modern through contemporary juxtapositions'. The emphasis is placed on talking and communicating to clients. As Project Orange explain in their office statement: 'We have ideas about how buildings are designed and we believe that these should be accessible to everybody who has an interest in the projects'.

This is narrative-propelled design: the designers compose a thematic or story directly out of the practice's understanding of the essential components of the brief. The themes are tailored to each project and so can vary greatly in their complexity. At the Citron Café in the Fitzwilliam Hotel in Dublin, for example, the thematic is a straightforward allusion to the 'citron' or lemon of the restaurant's title. The fruit is used throughout the interior to evoke connotations of Southern European warmth and freshness: the walls are citrus coloured – bright yellow and lime; the choice of materials is Mediterranean – there is white terrazzo on the floors; and even the lamp shades are inspired by the lemon's ovoid form.

In Delhi Deli, a chain of Indian takeaways by Project Orange, which had its first site opening in South London this summer, the thematic is less literal and more dynamic than that of Citron. It is described by Soane as 'the collision of the

traditional and modern Indias'. In its richly textured interior and exterior surfaces, the colourful kitsch of 21st-century India is artfully played off against traditional patterning and handcrafted detailing: the facade appears at first glance as a modern metallic box, though on closer inspection it is a layer of handcrafted zinc petals cut to a profile derived from Mogul designs; and the inside is lined with frenzied patterns, juxtaposed with brick-tiled floors and woven-front counters.

Project Orange's main tool for communicating these thematics to clients is the 'mood board'. This is a montage of images that conveys the potential 'feel' of a scheme, providing a glimpse of the sort of styles and components that it may include. A conscious bid for legibility, it abandons the specialist media of the architect – the drawing or the computer-generated image – in favour of the sort of visual language people encounter in their everyday lives through magazines and TV.

The original mood board for the up-market pizza takeaway Basilico, for example, features a number of pictures of cookers. This highlights the wood-burning oven with its stainless-steel mouth, which is the main culinary and design focus of the shops. The selection of images featuring natural or rustic materials anticipates the use of rough oak for panelling and benches in the final scheme; and the inclusion of a snapshot of a girl in sunglasses says something more far-reaching about the desire to make this a sophisticated and metropolitan outfit.

Where food is involved, the menu is an essential starting point for this process. (In addition to their restaurant work, Project Orange have under way a number of domestic projects and a large-scale scheme for a hotel in Chelsea.) For Soane, the relationship between food and design in a restaurant is integral. To succeed at a high level, a restaurant has to be strong on all counts, which includes design, food and service. The menu thus often provides essential food for thought. When the architects at Project Orange began work on Delhi Deli, they got together and cooked a curry made

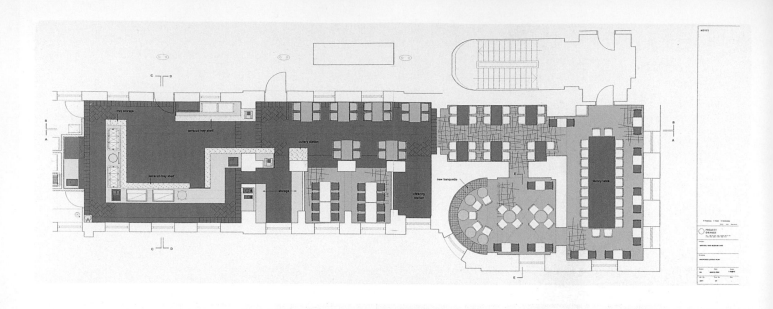

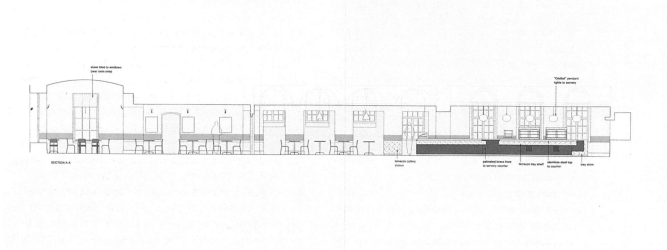

AUSTERITY GLAMOUR

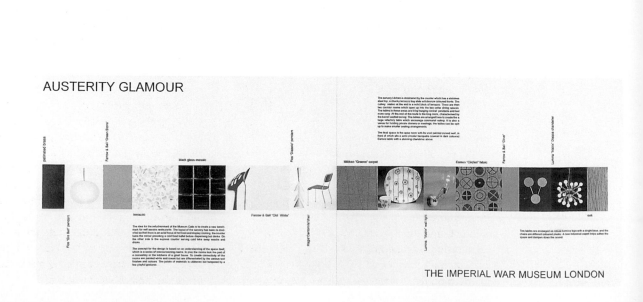

THE IMPERIAL WAR MUSEUM LONDON

from ingredients supplied by the clients. This emphasis on making set the tone for the entire project, opening up ideas about the way things are made in India. This resulted in the rich patterning of the interior and exterior and the earthy contrast of the brick floors; made out of clay, the brick also refers to the clay oven that gives such a decisive flavour to the food.

Alternatively, when a design concept has preceded the menu, it can exert its own influence over the food. When Project Orange devised 'Austerity Glamour' as the thematic for the café at the Imperial War Museum in London, it was apparent that bangers and mash were going to be more appropriate fare for a play on postwar culture than burgers and fries.

At a point when restaurant design seems to be more about producing fashionable scenery for the clientele – a trend epitomised by the lavish refurbishment of Mayfair eatery Cecconi's by Madonna's favoured designer David Collins – this all seems to be going against the grain. However, it is an approach that for James Soane has been formulated through a long period of informal collaboration and now a formalised partnership with Christopher Ash, and tested out through his professional experience.

Until 2001, Soane was a director at Conran and Partners. Here he led a number of fit-outs and construction projects around the world, including two major projects in Tokyo – Kamiyamacho, a new-build luxury housing project, and the Ark Hills Club and Spa. When discussing Gustavino's, the bar and restaurant at Bridgemarket in New York, which he also worked on for Conran's, he couches it in similar

terms to his Project Orange work. Occupying a huge site beneath the Queensboro Bridge, the restaurant, he explains, took its 'narrative' from its site and location. On a huge scale, it had the 'condition of being an inner landscape' with its own 'beach and deck' – the deck being the timber-clad mezzanine for formal dining that floats above the main interior space or 'beach'.

The success of Project Orange's approach has been most visibly borne out in London by its concept design for Basilico. Since the original two the client has developed the brand and rolled out a further three in London (Chelsea, Swiss Cottage and Highgate). As an up-market pizza takeaway, it has filled the gap in the home-delivery market for those who want quality food fast. The thin-crusted pizzas, baked in wood-burning ovens, are made from fresh ingredients often garnished with rocket. On the high street, these culinary aspirations are expressed by the fact that Basilico has the presence of a restaurant rather than a takeaway. Design elements, such as the black and white chequerboard floor, the distinctive green colour scheme of the basil-leaf logo designed by Studio Myerscough, and the substantial deli-style counter, mark it out as stylish and Italian.

Reinvented or recast as a building type of Italian descent, Basilico has left behind the homogeneity of the Anglo-American pizza chain, and this is a leap which Soane and Ash are set to make again with Delhi Deli. Looking to contemporary India for inspiration, they have reached beyond the established anglicised genre of the local Indian restaurant with its flocked wallpaper, dark interior and ornate light fittings. Delhi Deli's flip-up canopy and display hatch puts the cooking station on display and likens it to the kiosks of the Indian street vendor – the emphasis being placed on food being prepared before your eyes. ᐃ

Opposite top and middle
Plan and elevation of the café at the Imperial War Museum, London.

Opposite bottom
Mood board for the Imperial War Museum.

Above
Basilico, Lavender Hill, completed in 1999. Project Orange devised the original concept for the chain and oversaw the completion of the first two units in Lavender Hill and Fulham Road.

Cuisine

and Architecture:
A Recipe for a Wholesome Diet

Architects, like chefs, turn the raw into the cooked, transforming basic materials into an end product. **Sarah Wigglesworth** pursues the analogy between cooking and construction through food preparation and building to vernacular traditions and globalisation.

In building we refer to one type of cladding as a sandwich panel – two outside layers buttered with a filling. In the UK, a 'doorstep' is a very thick slice of bread, and we often refer to frivolous ornament as 'icing'. Recipes often begin with cutting, grinding, sifting or mixing, and so does building construction. In both, precise quantities of ingredients are measured out and combined; emulsions, suspensions, evaporations and chemical reactions are ways by which different materials unite. Concrete work resembles cake making, the only difference being the process of curing/baking.

Cuisine and architecture have more in common than one might at first believe. At the simplest level, architecture and cookery are both cultural processes. Cookery, like construction, takes nature and makes it into culture. At a very basic level, culture refers to the medium in which simple organisms (bacterial, fungal) can grow. Foodstuffs are a part of this world: yoghurt, yeast, cheese. But culture also refers to the more sophisticated ways in which techniques are employed and elements are combined to create a unique artefact. There is something which is chemical, and alchemical, in this transformation.[1] In both cuisine and architecture, a sensory and social world opens up from the perfect combination of elements brought together in time and space. The two practices answer the mere necessities of life, shelter and food, but both can transcend the prosaic to reach a higher level of culture.

All building is like cookery in the sense that it makes use of raw ingredients and combines them in particular and acceptable combinations, synthesising them into a product greater than the sum of the individual parts. In cooking we call this a meal, in architecture a building. Historically, architecture has extracted materials formed geologically or agriculturally and has worked them into something capable of construction – sheet metal, timber planks, glass panels, mineral fibre, slates. Food is grown –

also extracting nutrients from the soil – and transformed from the raw ingredient into something appetitive and recognisably edible. These two techniques manipulate the basic raw ingredient into other forms capable of recognition as building/food. Indeed, the very same product can constitute an edible *and* a building product: hemp and corn are just two examples. So, in a straw-bale building, corn is winnowed to extract the seed for making into bread and the remaining straws are baled up to become walling/insulation.

In preparing a *puttanesca* sauce, we take oil, garlic, tomatoes, anchovies, capers and olives and combine them in a particular sequence over the stove. The traditions of regional, even local cooking techniques influence the character and development of historically vernacular cuisines. In this way, the plant and equipment used, the special culinary know-how shared within a community and the ingredients specific to a climatic region unite to produce the unique flavour, colour and texture of a region's gastronomy.

The same could be said of building. Locally available materials were extracted and combined in ways which were developed over a long period of time, giving regional character to particular forms of construction. At the moment when techniques and styles are sufficiently identifiable they can be codified through their adherence to their unique characteristics. The shift from vernacular know-how to a codified record (recipe/specification) signifies a solidification – from an organic live art to a predetermined standard. It also implies a shift from control of knowledge transmitted orally and demonstrably by women (who by convention have prepared food) to the control, through rationalisation and codification of procedures, by men.

It is through this method that we have come to codify great cuisines – as we do great architectures – by their identification with such classificatory systems. The status of a great world cuisine/great world architecture is the highest accolade this value system can confer.

In reality, such classifications are historically and economically determined, subject to shifting influences and social conditions. The introduction of tomatoes from the New World into Europe was to revolutionise the diet of an entire continent. Likewise, Marco Polo's trip to China brought back the noodle, something which we now associate first and foremost with Italy. Absorbed into the native cuisine, these

external influences led to a redefinition of the country's culinary arts.

Similar events have taken place in the world of architecture,[2] yet until recently, culturally specific ways of building have not been readily transplanted. This has changed with the advent of global industrialisation, which has seen the mass production and distribution of standardised building components. Building products are now made by international companies, and the same products are now to be found in builders' merchants and DIY superstores throughout the world. This has become the modern building vernacular. Similarly, the ready-made meal or takeaway is surely the equivalent of the flat-pack or the mobile home, delivered in a form ready to consume.

Global capitalism is having a profound effect on the nature of both food and architecture. Increasingly, food in the West is being grown genetically and is manipulated, modified or manufactured into sophisticated, value-added products for home consumption. Determined by the requirements of transportation, shelf life and visual appeal, fresh supermarket vegetables are selectively cultivated to a perfect shape and colour, are prewashed, presorted, chopped and bagged up so that they no longer resemble the raw ingredient from which they were derived. From brewing and preserving to meat, vegetables and fruit, our choice is being limited and standardised in the name of consumer demand.[3] Research shows that children in inner cities have little idea of where their food comes from or how it is produced (Where does milk come from? – bottles, of course!). The rise in sales of precooked 'convenience' foods is producing a generation of people who don't know how to cook, and is spawning a variety of cookery manuals returning to the basics.[4]

As the building world too has been increasingly dominated by industrialised production, we have witnessed new methods of construction ranging from system building and prefabrication to the development of large components which come with full design specification, subcontracting skills (supply and fix) and a lifetime guarantee. Typically this sort of operation takes place on an multinational scale. Such global blanding (sic) permits scant room for local specificity or respect for the traditions developed over centuries which ground building to its place. From windows to sheet metal, from bricks to cast stone, someone in a factory somewhere, usually distant from us, is preparing a product for incorporation into our next design. Like the work of the short-order cook, the designer's role now essentially consists in combining these products in different ways: design freedom is limited to choosing colours or finishes. Skill is measured by the freshness and novelty of these juxtapositions within the canon of accepted good taste.

Opposite
The Straw House, 2001.
Detail of straw-bale walling.

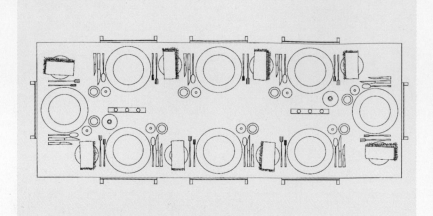

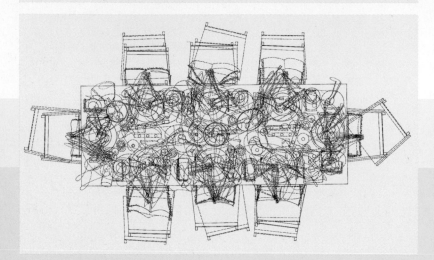

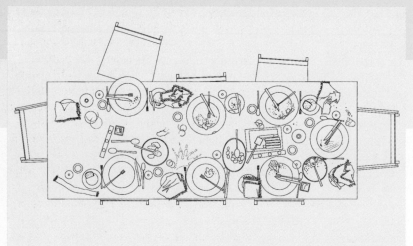

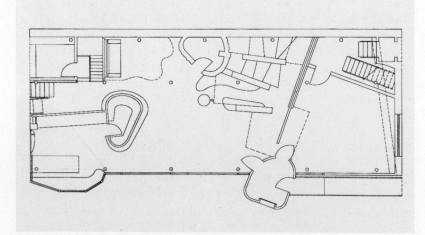

Similarly, in the world of *haute cuisine,* it now takes millions of pounds to establish a restaurant which aims to play on the international stage (achieving those coveted Michelin rosettes), so successful chefs increasingly need financial backers. Since a large investment is required, risks are high and the winners are frequently those acquired by larger conglomerates – umbrella organisations that own several brand identities. At the highest end in both cooking and building, brand identity is reinforced by the superstar chef/architect.[5] Long, hard apprenticeships, sometimes in dull pubs and catering schools, are the equivalent of the design *charettes* and night-time toil that make up the average architecture student's educational experience. The engine for this sacrifice is the belief in the possibility of becoming an Albert Roux or a Norman Foster. Interestingly, virtually without exception these superstars are male. The cook/architect women are the unsung heroines working quietly in the background.

Between globalising tendencies on the one hand and branded high-art chef/architect genius on the other, there is nonetheless a middle way. A TV 'lad-chef' like Jamie Oliver – very different from the didactic Delia – treats recipes with irreverence, using approximate measures and altering them according to available ingredients and his personal fancy. Pleasure, resourcefulness, invention and opportunism are the characteristics of this relaxed cuisine. The key feature of this approach is that the cook/eater is a participant in the making of the meal, amending and adjusting the recipe according to taste or budget. He or she is not mystified by technique or in thrall to the superstar chef.

By analogy, there is a kind of architecture which does not slavishly adhere to predetermined specifications,[6] materials or techniques; rather, it uses these as a base from which to invent, and is similarly opportunistic, irreverent, organic and approximate. In the case of such a participatory or approximate architecture, the user and architect blur, and standard methods become productive arenas where invention and convention clash to create new and unexpected possibilities.

An important distinction exists in the relationship between the production of a meal/building and its consumption. While architects often resemble chefs, the diner is more likely to resemble the user of a building. In the same way that a chef relinquishes control once the meal is delivered to the table, so an architect can no longer control the reception of his or her work after handover. The rituals of dining resonate in the codified behaviour of people performing their roles in public places. But the reception of a meal, as with the reception of a building, depends on many other factors, not all of which lie within the control of the maker or social convention.

In many ways the direct and unmediated cooking process helps to clarify intentions (the chef probably

Right
The Straw House roof garden.

Middle
The Straw House productive/
ornamental garden.

Far right
The Straw House at dusk.

Opposite
The dining table and first-floor
plan of the Straw House:
A: The lay of the table
B: The meal
C: The trace of the meal
D: The plan of the house

Notes
1. On this subject, see 'The
Culinary Connection: an
analysis and comparison of
architecture and cookery',
unpublished dissertation by
Lance Routh, University of
Sheffield, October 2000.
2. For example, the advent and
absorption of Classicism into
British architecture in the 17th
century.
3. Food retailers such as
McDonald's, Burger King and
the Nestlé Corporation have
developed a reputation for a
standardised product that one
can be sure of buying
anywhere throughout the
world.
4. The recent books of Britain's
most popular TV cook, Delia
Smith, cover such topics as
how to boil an egg.
5. Frank Gehry, Rem Koolhaas
and Zaha Hadid are all
examples of the globally
branded star, as are chefs like
Marco Pierre White.
6. There is a clear similarity
between the recipe and the
National Building Specification
(NBS). But where a recipe is not
policed and monitored, and is
therefore more open to
interpretation and invention,
the NBS is a legal document
which requires strict
compliance. However, this
does not mean that it cannot
be reinvented, rephrased,
whatever.
7. Nico Ladenis and Gordon
Ramsay – Brtiain's three-
rosette Michelin chefs – are
renowned for verbally abusing
guests whose attitude to their
work displeases them. Some
diners have even been asked
to leave the restaurant.

administers his or her kitchen, and may even prepare his or her own dishes), yet building is almost always mediated through the hands of a contractor, producing another level of separation between designer and consumer. Those dishes touched by the hand of the famous chef deserve reverence, so much so that some chefs are known to abuse diners who fail to display sufficient piety.[7] By corollary, the punishment meted out by their architectural equivalent is to suffer the oppressingly wilful and overdeterministic inventions of the egotistical architect.

Such a thesis feeds into the thinking behind a project recently completed by Sarah Wigglesworth Architects: the Straw House. The narrative of the house was derived from an awareness of how the rituals of eating played out on the plane of the dining table are similar to the rituals of domestic life as depicted in the plan of a dwelling. The manner in which the guests sitting round a table interact during the course of a meal can be compared to the way in which people interact in the space of a house. Everyone around a table obeys social rules, just as we do in life, and the movement of props during the dinner – plates, glasses, cutlery, serving dishes, napkins, cruet set – all describe particular relationships and events in time. So it is with the space of architecture. Furniture, walls, columns and stairs all frame our physical and social movement, and act as markers for the rituals we perform every day. The drawings of the table top describe how similar these ideas are, in space and time, and link the table top with the plan form of the Straw House.

Extending the analogy, the house has walls of straw, something which makes explicit the architecture's connection with food production. It has been argued above that the working of metals extracted from the ground, the growing, felling and sawing of timber for the floors, walls and roof, even the burning and slaking of lime and the mixing of it with sand to form render, are processes in a productive continuum, and differ from cookery merely in respect of their edibility. Only the chemically engineered components begin to depart from this rule.

At a more prosaic level the house itself is productive and exists in a productive landscape. The roof, with its garden, is the host to mustard and wild strawberries, while the garden combines edible and ornamental species indiscriminately. Apple and damson trees are espaliered against an old south wall (they form a sort of woven textile), while lettuces, carrots and beetroot are planted among alliums, poppies and roses. Potatoes are grown not just for their tubers but for their dark green foliage and white flowers. Not much here is inedible. Kitchen waste is composted and the dry toilet does the same with the human variety. The manure that results from both processes can be used to fertilise the garden, completing the cycle.

The Straw House is an example of an approximate architecture. In this project the form of contract was reinvented, using a productive, partnering (non-adversarial) method of collaboration. We used the project to expand the palette of conventionally available materials, extending them into organic and local productive arenas, and invented new recipes for combining those ingredients. Much of this work consisted in taking available handed-down knowledge and reworking it into methods suited to the UK climate and regulatory framework. In such a process, materials become reclassified and traditional know-how combines with new technologies to form delicious new formulations. We have found that at our premises in Stock Orchard Street, the relationship between hearth, the traditional cooking site, and home are unexpectedly and refreshingly reappraised. △

Helen Castle is Editor of *Architectural Design*. Since joining the editorial staff at Wiley-Academy in 1999, she has steered the magazine in a new direction. She has collaborated with Christian Küsters of CHK Design and Mariangela Palazzi Williams, Senior Production Editor at Wiley-Academy, on reformatting and redesigning the publication. Helen has a BA in Art History and Architecture from the University of East Anglia and an MSc in History of Modern Architecture and Theory from the Bartlett.

Gabrielle Esperdy is an architectural historian whose work examines the intersection of modern architecture and popular culture, primarily in the US. She is especially interested in the 20th-century commercial landscape and the critical analysis of the social and spatial practices of shopping and selling. She received a BA from Smith College and a PhD from the City University of New York. She is an Assistant Professor in the School of Architecture at the New Jersey Institute of Technology.

Karen A Franck is a Professor at the New Jersey Institute of Technology, where she teaches in the School of Architecture and the Department of Humanities and Social Science. Since receiving a PhD in environmental psychology from the City University of New York, she has pursued her interest in design and everyday life in various ways. Her two edited books focus on housing and the idea of type in architecture, while *Architecture Inside Out* (Wiley-Academy, 2000), written with Bianca Lepori, takes the form of a manifesto.

Samantha Hardingham was trained at the Architectural Association. *London: A Guide to Recent Architecture* (Ellipsis, 1994), written during her diploma year at the AA, is approaching a sixth edition. *Eat London: Architecture and Eating* (Ellipsis, 1996) was published following her involvement in setting up Crowbar Coffee, two coffee bars in north London known for their radical approach to combining design, food and architectural events. She is currently editing a book on the architect Cedric Price.

Jamie Horwitz PhD is Associate Professor of Architecture and teaches interdisciplinary studios and seminars in the graduate programme at Iowa State University. She has a regular feature on architectural issues in the *Des Moines Register*, and her recent work has appeared in the journals *Thresholds*, *Forum* and *Places*. In 2001 she and Paulette Singley received a Graham Foundation Grant to publish *Eating Architecture* (MIT Press, 2003), a collection of essays on the spatiality of food and the taste of architecture.

Stephan Marc Klein is the 2000/2001 Institute Professor/Distinguished Teacher in the Graduate Interior Design Department at Pratt Institute. He founded and co-teaches the department's thesis level course on the design and planning of museum-based interpretative exhibitions. Stephan received the 2002 Michael Tatum Award for Excellence in Education from the International Interior Design Association. An architect with a PhD in environmental psychology, he is writing a book on the theory and history of museum exhibition design.

Jayne Merkel is a contributing editor to *Architectural Design*. The former editor of *Oculus* magazine in New York, she is currently writing a monograph on Eero Saarinen for Phaidon Press.

Mark Morris is a lecturer at the Bartlett and Architectural Association. Trained as an architect at the Ohio State University, he is currently completing his dissertation on scale models with the London Consortium, University of London. Awarded a study grant from the RIBA in 2000, he is a research fellow at Tate Modern and reviews books on art, architecture and food for *Contemporary* magazine.

Sheridan Rogers is a journalist, author, broadcaster and food stylist in Sydney. She has written four books, including *The Cook's Garden* (HarperCollins, 1992) and *Seasonal Entertaining* (HarperCollins, 1994). In recognition of her contributions to food writing, she has received several awards, among them the Award for Gastronomic Writing in 1992. Chapters from Sheridan's latest book are posted on her web site at *www.sheridanrogers.com*.

Masaaki Takahashi is a freelance journalist and critic in Tokyo who writes on design, culture and architecture. After completing his university education in Tokyo, he studied fine art in Berlin and interior design at the Polytechnic of North London and the Fashion Institute of Technology in New York. Masaaki plans to write entertaining and enlightening essays on subculture, architecture and urban planning in contemporary Japan.

Sarah Wigglesworth is principal of Sarah Wigglesworth Architects. The goal of the practice is to make buildings that employ readily available materials in inventive ways. The most well-known demonstration of this approach is the award-winning Straw House and Quilted Office in north London. The practice recently completed the Clearwater Garden at the Chelsea Flower Show and is currently working on arts and housing projects and a school building, in collaboration with artist Susan Collins.

Below
Apple's New York City computer store, in SoHo transforms the
former Prince Street post office into a sunny shopping arcade
entirely devoted to selling the company's newest products.

Below left
The monumental stair in the Apple megastore in SoHo, built of luminous
floating glass treads without risers, is pinned between supporting walls of clear
structural glass.

Below right
The minimalist sky window consists of insulated glass panels that have been
fritted with a barely perceptible sunscreen. Signage marks the 'genius bar',
a help desk staffed with computer experts.

Apple Core Values

Apple Computers holds a well-deserved reputation for being a top trendsetters in terms of consumer appeal. The company's very wantable recent machines, with glamorous transparent keyboards or titanium cases, win consistent raves from devotees beyond the usual fraternity of tech heads. For Apple, superior external design and presentation have fanned the flames of mass-consumer desire. **Craig Kellogg** contrasts two high-street shops built recently to showcase Apple products – each store an extreme in its attitude towards the history and marketing of new-tech gadgetry.

Below
Sturdy Parsons' tables in the Apple megastore display
computers for sale under a shimmering ceiling system that
mixes incandescent down-lights with luminous panels.

While still sheathed in shipping Styrofoam, the current crop of Apple computers is no less catatonic than any of the unplugged metal-and-plastic boxes that competitors bundle into big corrugated cartons overseas. Even after the various offerings from computer manufacturers are unpacked and powered up, meaningful differences become comprehensible to only a tiny minority of nerds. So the race for new customers has encouraged Apple designers to think outside the box. They've poured effort into flashy industrial design that differentiates Apple products at a glance. And a complementary campaign has opened proprietary Apple boutiques in upscale shopping districts across America.

To style the new stores, company co-founder Steve Jobs engaged veteran architect Peter Bohlin. At first blush, Bohlin seems an unlikely choice, given his reputation for residential designs in recycled wood, but he was involved in the legendary mansion for Microsoft guru Bill Gates, and also worked on a house and offices for Jobs (who personally attended store-planning meetings). Starting with a template for smaller boutiques in shopping centres, Bohlin, with New York architect Ronnette Riley, planned the Apple megastore for a key tourist corner in Manhattan's SoHo.

The result is nothing short of spectacular – an orderly but energetic showroom expensively finished in frosted metal. The silken floors are stone, while a linear skylight of fritted glass hovers over the atrium. At street level, beefy maple (and maple veneer) Parsons tables are heaped with computers offering uncensored Internet access. On the upper level, at the summit of a grand structural-glass staircase, are an informal theatre for seminars, a software library and a children's zone with computers on a low white table encircled by small black bean-shaped poufs.

This unflinching futurism in SoHo could not contrast more strongly with the Tekserve store, which opened at around the same time. Tekserve is a repair service and Apple-authorised retailer that bills itself as 'The Old Reliable Macintosh Shop'. Two decades ago, it was launched by Mac enthusiasts in a living room on the upper floor of a loft building nearby (the new store is their first at street level). And although 'Sex and the City' has visited Tekserve, the target market is clearly nerds. One large wall at the front is nearly consumed by a stunning mass of poly-packed

cords and connectors hanging in slack rows. The lighting
is harsh metal-halide, like a gymnasium. But the ceiling
is painted sky blue and the floor is new, if inexpensive,
varnished oak. Surface-mounted ductwork overhead and
exposed brick walls contribute to the easy, functional charm
of the place.

Co-owner Dick Demenus designed the $1 million Tekserve
renovation himself and invested the store with a sense of
history. The store promotes a messy sense of community
by invoking nostalgia for the glories of Apple's past. A dingy
hooked craft-rug in the stairwell displays Apple's now-
abandoned logo with rainbow stripes. Early radios line high
shelves. Waiting customers help themselves to Cokes in
glass bottles, dispensed by an old-fashioned coin-operated
machine. And Demenus says there's more clutter to come –
an antique printing press, for example, is destined for the
area devoted to ink-jet printers.

You don't hear much these days about the debate between
advocates for vernacular design – the architecture-without-
architects crowd – versus corporate designers. In the
backlash against Postmodernism, professionals have mostly
given up trying to imitate the locals. Meanwhile, vernacular

folk like Demenus don't give a damn about established
principles of retailing. To find a computer that you can
touch and buy in his store, you have to walk deep
inside. At the front, inside the glass windows where you
might expect to see beckoning displays of shiny new
machines for sale, is a large corkboard for community
notices posted by customers.

A bulletin board in the vestibule might also improve
Apple SoHo – but it would be entirely out of character.
The SoHo boutique looks so bold and welcoming
precisely because it aims to encourage the uninitiated
to drop in and test-drive a titanium PowerBook. History
and local culture were downplayed in the design.

With two such opposite strategies, Apple ultimately
needs Tekserve as much as Tekserve needs Apple. The
SoHo store may attract customers but Tekserve keeps
them – and does their dirty work. Even while Jobs
polishes brave new retail offerings to exhibit in his ultra-
modern showcase, a hundred broken old Apples await
repair on Demenus's industrial shelving – alongside
the ancient Coke machine and Bakelite radios that
were once new and glittering in their own heyday. ⚞

111 +

The Müchener Rück Headquarters

Jeremy Melvin looks at a new building in Munich by Baumschlager
and Eberle that defies the usual architectural categories of
Expressionism and Rationalism. Expanding on a great tradition
of Central European architecture, it is 'about illusion and fantasy
– as well as enormously skilful construction'.

Right, top
Skilful massing and the hint of a traditional material like stone allow the new building to relate to its traditionally designed neighbours.

Right, middle
The interplay of the serrated effect of the canted glass and strong horizontal lines contrasts with the building's *Jugendstil* neighbour.

Below, bottom
From another angle the frameless glass of the outer facade assumes the character of a continuous sheet.

Below left
Site plan. The plan form manipulates and extends the patchwork of small open spaces in the centre of the city block.

Below right
Floor plans. Ground Floor (*Erdgeschoss*). Occupying the building's perimeter, the offices wrap around a central armature of the extraordinary entrance foyer.

First floor (*Obergeschoss*). The entrance foyer is double height, with a bridge across at first-floor level.
Floors 2–4 (*Regelgeschoss*). Within the German expectations of cellular rather than open-plan offices, the floor plates make efficient use of space with easy access to outside views and ventilation.
Top floor (*Attikageschoss*). Breaking through the rationalised discipline of the lower levels are two free-flowing attic floors.

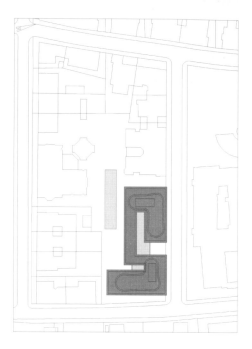

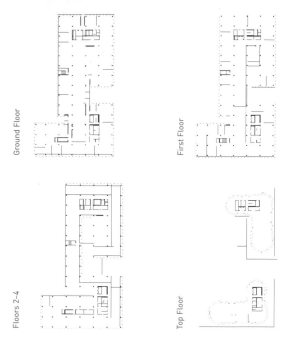

Nothing comes closer to undermining that complacent little corner of Anglo-American architectural historiography, which splits the world into mutually exclusive categories of Expressionism and Rationalism than the work of contemporary Austrian architects like Baumschlager and Eberle. At first glance their headquarters of the Müchener Rück insurance company in Munich looks like Mies out of Egon Eiermann, firmly on the R side of the Great Divide. But old Egon didn't normally place his panes of glass at an angle to the facade line, and he generally sealed the gaps between them. The amorphous forms of the attic storey might have seemed an unnecessary indulgence, and his interiors did not use the craft of carpentry to create the surreal impression of a pixellated computer-generated image. This is more than rationalised expression, or expressed rationality; it is a balance between craft and digital technology, between order and freedom, tradition and the future, or as B+E themselves put it, between 'man and nature' – and it is one which our little historiographical conceit finds very difficult.

This is because dividing architecture into Expressionism and Rationalism fits very neatly with the assumption that architectural debate is framed around a relationship between form and function. It holds that Rationalists are about form and nothing else, while Expressionists update the concept of Functionalism, with a little help from Sandy Wilson's 'Other Tradition' and a quote from Ludwig Wittgenstein: 'meaning lies in use'. Although this might fit with puritanical Anglo-Saxon prejudices, it hardly does justice to that great tradition of Central European architecture which is about illusion and fantasy – as well as enormously skilful construction – that dates at least from Vierzehnheiligen. Armed with Wittgenstein, a Central European who found England more congenial than

his place of birth, everything from Bavarian baroque plasterwork to the ornate interiors of Hoffmann or Olbrich has no meaning as it has no use. Just as the Central European tradition has a long history, so the narrow English view goes back to Pugin, whose contradictory liking for pinnacles and belief that architectural features could only be justified by convenience, construction and propriety might neatly be resolved were he impaled on one. That would certainly be convenient, constructive and propitious.

What makes the work of B+E especially piquant here is that they almost turn these narrow prejudices on themselves. They are masters of form in that mnemonic, typological sense where particular forms carry associations and meanings that transcend function, but show as much invention as any expressive Functionalist. They use that most traditional (especially in Austria) of building materials – timber – but force it to such visual and constructive extremes that it conveys many more associations than the simple expression of its construction.

The austere rigour of the Müchener Rück facades might superficially refer to the postwar tradition of office buildings or that simplistic *Bundesrepublik* truism that transparency is somehow associated with democracy. The building contrasts with its rather tokenistically *Jugendstil* neighbour, simultaneously intriguing and inscrutable. The edge of the canted glass panes might, from a distance, be the sort of stainless-steel tie rods that grace so many outer walls in the British 'hi-tech' tradition; but this building's flamboyant effect comes from far fewer components. Close to, the

richer reflections which nonparallel layers of glass give is certainly Expressionistic. It might almost be a glass version of Fritz Hoeger's extraordinary Chilehaus in Hamburg though the horizontal lines, emphasised with a simple metal trim, call such wilfulness to order.

But the simple, unframed glass panes are also part of a sophisticated passive energy concept. All is not what it seems, or as B+E explain: 'Intelligent building technique is the organisation of the interaction between architecture and the environment'. Although this could stand for their general approach, they go on to define it in a specific sense: 'The goal is a building with an optimal dialogue between architecture and the environment warmed and lit by the sun, cooled by the earth and aired by the wind'. This aim is clearest in the facade construction. Four-fifths of the outer wall is glass, with the outermost layer a series of frameless sheets set at a slight angle to leave a small gap between each. Behind is an interstitial layer trapping heat but allowing excess warmth to escape, while roller blinds increase the protection from solar gain. Heating and cooling, maximising the use of thermal mass, comes through the floor, while the fresh air comes through the facade. However, various passive measures and heat recovery systems reduce heat loss through ventilation by 25 per cent. None of this is especially new in principle; what B+E do is to bring the existing ideas to a pitch of refinement and to find a visual idiom which expresses it within that refined sensibility. As the outer leaves of glass are not the wall of the offices, they are not encumbered with frames or spandrel panels; they rest directly on horizontal elements which are in effect solar shades, though they do not resemble the normal messy angled louvres.

Wrapped by the continuous outer wall, the building forms essentially into two wings at right-angles to each other with indentations to form small courtyards which link into the other residual spaces inside the city block. The office spaces, cellular and disciplined, are on the outside, each with its own piece of perimeter wall. Within, as a kind of compositional armature, is an extraordinary two-storey entrance foyer. Clad 'totally in wood', as Carlo Baumschlager explains, 'for atmosphere and quality of light', its strips, regular in size and finish but apparently random in tone, almost defy the material's tactile qualities and evoke, for example, the Expressionist use of glass bricks.

But this is also a contemporary version, as if in a pixellated computer-image of that age-old German phenomenon of the Forest, a place of mystery and danger but also, ultimately, offering the possibility of personal fulfilment. Even if timber clads every surface and forms the reception desk, the regularity of the blocks and almost heavenly light from above ensure this is a forest shorn of its terrors, where a magic bullet has already killed the resident demon.

Baumschlager adds that the wood suggests 'something beyond the walls', as if the experience of this forest is only a formative stage; the real work goes on behind the wall. And if the insurance transactions that once demanded forest-threatening quantities of paper now take place largely on computers, this only makes the pixellated effect of the timber even more appropriate. Here the traditional material turns on itself to suggest the fragmentation of the present and hope for the future. The sterile debate between form and function is transcended into an expression of ideas. ◬

Johnson Chou
Architects

Johnson Chou is an architect whose minimalist language of formal reductivism belies broader preoccupations with space and the perceptual. **Sean Stanwick** describes how, through his engagement with other media and his work on small-scale projects, Chou has turned the unpromising economic climate in Canada to his advantage.

French existentialist Maurice Merleau-Ponty proposed a single state of being between what he called the body-subject and its environment. In contemplating the transformation and perception of the self, he wrote: 'As one enters, a position becomes situation, becomes subject, becomes playground, becomes oneself'. This action of creating a oneness between body, space and experience is a moment Toronto architect Johnson Chou feels most comfortable in. In just a few short years he has developed a portfolio of internationally recognised work that transcends mere Functionalism and has come to embody that which Ponty sought to resolve.

Since founding his firm in 1999, the 39-year-old, Taiwan-born Chou has focused his attention primarily on multidisciplinary projects, particularly those that challenge the spatial and perceptual differences between object and subject, stasis and mobility, observation and participation. With a staff of five, including associate and personal friend Steffanie Adams, creative forays have included architecture; interior, industrial, graphic and product design; and multimedia presentations.

While Chou's work may appear on first reading as dependent on the often clichéd devices of minimalism, nothing could be further from the truth. His working methodology is both logical and yet somehow paradoxical. Adhering to an intentionally rigorous process of reduction in search of what he calls the elemental, Chou presents an architecture that is, on the surface, pure in its expression and form. But to say that the crisp minimalist lines are the end result belies the depth of his paradigm. The progeny of his methodical distillation is, in fact, an enterprise of perpetual transformation. 'Slidetiltpivot', the title of his retrospective exhibition (Toronto, 2001) – which at first seems a product of rhetorical archispeak – is actually his modus operandi. Acting as patterns of mobility by which multiplicity of function is furthered, Slide, Tilt and Pivot establish a fundamental relationship between operation and function, whereby the action of one begets the other and vice versa. Spaces and forms continually shape-shift as fixtures slide to change their orientation; walls tilt to become work surfaces and counters pivot to serve as room dividers. Although this creates a deceptively complex system of animated layers, it is only through the exploration of these layers that the operational possibilities of the elemental become fully realised.

Welcoming the opportunity to deliver an object or space that can challenge the dichotomies between singularity of form and multiplicity of function, Chou says: 'I try to pare down my spaces to the bare essentials ... but then I try to create elements within the space that provoke interest'. To support this approach he has intentionally kept his material palette sparse. Limited, yet opportunity rich, polished stainless steel, frosted glass and wood have remained his three standards. 'One of my concerns is that Modernism can be too cold,' he says, as he explains his use of natural and stained veneers for balance and warmth. 'I've always admired the work of John Pawson,' he continues, citing the British ultra-Minimalist as a strong aesthetic influence.

Chou also draws references from the mechanically sophisticated Russian Constructivists and their early theatrical stage sets. Indeed, he uses his filmic control of light with choreographed perfection to bring otherwise static objects to life. In a wholly visceral manner, Chou theatricises the simple act of window-shopping by putting both the product and shopper on display, suspending them in a temporal state of theatrical animation. While it's no secret that the power of seduction lies less in the revealed than in the act of revealing, it is also no coincidence that Chou's work approaches the theatrical and embraces the erotic. In much the same way as Gypsy Rose Lee used striptease as a tool for sensory titillation, Chou intentionally exploits our voyeuristic tendencies. With each illuminated layer and subsequent exposure, he leaves us in a state of excited anticipation of what delights lie beneath each translucent veil.

Graduating from the University of Waterloo, one of Canada's premier architecture schools, Chou's early work history was enviable. Landing coveted design positions with top-ranking firms including Arthur Erickson, Parkin Architects and the late Ernest Annau, he was involved in several high-profile projects including the Canadian Chancellery in Washington DC. Unfortunately, the recession of the late 1980s would leave Chou with an indelible mark of pessimism. Like many in the field, he rapidly became disillusioned with a 'profession that was in decline, characterised by firms with an apparent disinterest in design, and supported by clients who were only interested in the bottom line. As soon as the design was done, the designers were the first to be let go'.

With little in the way of steady work, Chou sought other vehicles for his creative expression. In 1996 he partnered with Montreal-based film-production designer Patricia Christie to form Archive Inc, a walk-in commercial art gallery and comprehensive image database. With a catalogue of over 10,000 digital items, Archive displays and sources the images of over 500 Canadian artists to the film, television and graphic design industry. In typical fashion, the interior of the 80-square-metre space does double duty as well. A cantilevered horizontal wood plane defines the reception area while an illuminated Plexiglas wall screens the administration spaces and is also an upright light table. During gallery showings, both pivot about vertical axes to allow free motion within an uninterrupted space. While Archive has successfully filled a niche in Toronto's growing film and media community, more importantly it served as a formative early venue for Chou's methodological experimentations with spatial transformation and manipulation.

On the strength of Archive, Chou was able to secure several interior commissions including Vizio, a hybrid optical boutique and contemporary photo gallery. Vizio, like much of Chou's work for that matter, shares with Archive the ability to transform itself to suit a variety of

Resumé

users' needs. In fact, Chou's talent for seamlessly integrating a duality of intent and performance when space is at an absolute premium has become his calling card. The TNT series – a collection of high-end speciality fashion stores including Man, Woman, Intimates and Blu – features illuminated diaphanous panels, translucent frosted walls that double as specialised display units, capsule-like changing cubicles and spring-tensioned, pivoting horizontal work surfaces that rotate to allow for product display.

At the smaller, more tangible scale, Chou has diversified into fixture and furniture design. Mr Greyson's Cabinet of Wonders, his hybrid storage-cum-worktable that won the Toronto Arts Council Protégé Award – is a luminescent *objet d'art* that seduces the user by skilfully peeling back its layers to reveal a mélange of translucent vitrines. Slide, a collection of light fixtures, features anodised aluminium floor, wall and table sconces, through which movable acrylic shades pivot both horizontally and vertically to allow task or ambient lighting. Designed for Eurolite, Slide won the Ontario Association of Architects Award in Artefacts category. Other projects include M1, a self-contained closable office work station; and Ubi – short for ubiquitous – a modular illuminated retail display system for New York-based Bernstein Display.

With each project, Chou seamlessly spans the creative disciplines and their respective scales, making it difficult to render even a cursory categorisation. Dancing between micro and macro, he thrives on the instability of the borderline, and leaves the traditional relationships of space to bodies, psyches and objects in a state of flux. Perhaps this is why he finds comfort in the words of Ponty: both a product and a purveyor of their context, his works intentionally inhabit the ambiguous zone and successfully absorb the difference to converge as one symbiotic moment of participatory experience. On discussing the point of convergence between art, architecture, interior design and even artefact, Chou readily admits that the borders are fundamentally interchangeable: 'I see it all being linked', he says, 'it's all about narrative for me, and bringing it all together … materials, space and people … is a necessary element in realising a unified whole'.

What's next for Chou? On the boards are several projects. He is currently dancing between Toronto and New York, finalising design details for a furniture showroom. Influenced by the work of Robert Irwin and the lighting of James Turrell, the project uses a series of suspended fabric layers as flexible room dividers. He also launched Womb at the 2002 Toronto Interior Design Show. Activated by mechanically automated furniture, lighting and interior fixtures, Womb brings him one step closer to realising fully transformable habitation. Like any architect though, what Chou would really like to do is a building. With the healthier economic Canadian climate and his rapidly expanding repertoire, it's unlikely that he will have to wait long.

Sean Stanwick is a Canadian freelance architectural writer based in Toronto. He has a particular interest in urban issues and the themed spectacular. A frequent contributor to AD, he was also a contributing author for *Sustaining Architecture in the Anti-Machine Age* and is currently writing *Winery Builders* (both Wiley-Academy). He works as a design architect at Salter Farrow Pilon Architects in Toronto.

1988	Graduated from the University of Waterloo, School of Architecture.
1996	Co-founded Archive Inc Gallery and Multimedia Digital Art Library. TNT clothing boutique, Toronto.
1998	Vizio Eyewear and Photo Gallery. Offices for multimedia design company, Medium One, Toronto. TNT Woman, TNT Man, TNT Intimates – Hazelton Lanes, Toronto.
1999	Founded Johnson Chou Design. UBI store fixture line for Bernstein Display, NY. Gold Award – Outstanding Booth Design, Interior Design Show, Toronto.
2000	Bernstein Display – new offices and showroom, Long Island, NY. Created Slide light fixture collection – Eurolite, Toronto.
2001	TNT – new boutiques for TNT Man, TNT Woman, TNT Blu. Toronto Arts Protégé Award – Commission for Mr Greyson's Cabinet of Wonders. Yolles Loft Residence, Toronto. Incorporated business and name change to Johnson Chou Inc.
2002	New showroom, Basics Furniture, NY. Nienkamper – production of multi-purpose furniture piece workplaysleep.01. Womb – Interior Design Show, Toronto. Ontario Association of Architects – Design Excellence Award. TNT Woman, Best of Canada Award (*Canadian Interiors* magazine).

Slide Light Fixtures

Vizio Eyewear and Photo Gallery

Slide is a collection of light fixtures, designed by Chou for Eurolite, which features anodised aluminium floor, wall and table sconces. Movable acrylic shades pivot both horizontally and vertically to allow task or ambient lighting.

Vizio Eyewear and Photo Gallery, Toronto, 1998

Vizio melds two functions that are both well defined and complementary: a photo gallery and a high-end eyewear boutique. The design for the 860-square-foot space employs a strong linear *parti* with movable elements and coordinated custom-designed fixtures. Celebrating the mechanics and materiality of eyewear, Chou employed his typical leitmotif: glass and stainless steel juxtaposed against neutral walls. The curved white wall containing eyewear displays, gently draws visitors from the street into the space and also allows for a fluidity of space and movement. Opened with the tap of the finger, eyewear displays consist of sliding stainless-steel trays and shelves, glass casings and removable protective glass screens. Furniture elements slide, tilt and pivot as fitting tables suspended from tracks, and swing out for use or in to create uninterrupted space for gallery showings. The tables and seating function as a focal point for movement through the space, while fitting tables slide along an overhead track to nestle beside a cushioned bench for gallery shows. Like a good pair of spectacles, the adjustable tables also feature stainless-steel angled recesses and an adjustable mirror that slides forward and back, and tilts to suit different customer sizes. This bifocal division of function is expressed in the orientation of the space as well; eyewear is displayed to the left, black-and-white photographs to the right.

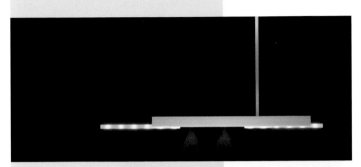

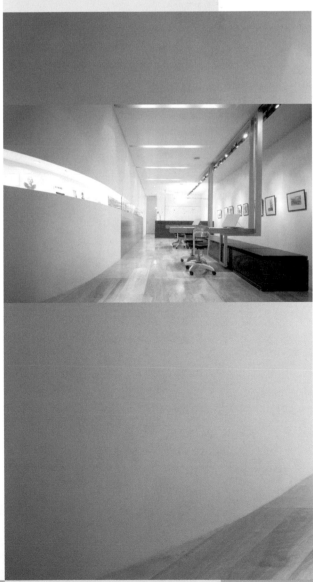

Yolles Loft Residence

Womb

Yolles Loft Residence, Toronto, 2001
While many US cities have already experienced a boom in loft conversions, Toronto's industrial revolution is just beginning. The 1000-square-foot Yolles Residence in the recently converted Merchandise Lofts is Chou's first residential project. The bulk of the interior alterations focused primarily on the bedroom and bath areas and included the design of custom millwork, fixtures and lighting. Chou immediately gutted the tightly divided space and replaced all nonstructural walls with sandblasted glass screens, clear glass vignettes and floor-to-ceiling sliding stainless-steel partitions that slide away from view to assimilate adjacent spaces. The bedroom and bath areas function as a single, uninterrupted space with the wet areas located on a stepped platform. Clad with textured slate, the platform features a cantilevered stainless-steel sculptural vanity to define the washing and bathing zones. Hidden behind the vanity is a step-down bath and shower clad with the same blue-green slate as the platform. The king-size bed, wrapped in a perimeter band of brushed aluminium, is cantilevered from the wall and appears to hover in mid-space. A wall of floor-to-ceiling storage cupboards, also finished in aluminium, runs the entire length of the bedroom and bathing areas and functions as a muted backdrop to the defining sculptural elements. Piercing the neutral white plane of the ceiling, two recessed bands of light provide linear definition of the loft's primary zones when the partitions are hidden from view. Halogen and fluorescent lighting is designed to strategically highlight existing and newly designed fixtures, and to be adjustable for changes in atmosphere and function.

Womb: work, office, meditation, base
Interior Design Show, Toronto, 2002
The notion of 'retreat' invokes more than simply escape. Away from our day-to-day chaos, retreats are where inspiration is cultivated. A multifunctional inhabitable space, Womb recognises that a place of refuge must service a variety of needs and functions. At various stages of transformation it exists as four separate rooms within one basic volume: kitchen/dining, work/office, bedroom/living and a Zen-like meditative environment. As sparse or as complex as desired, Womb's automated elements create a 21st-century 'machine for living' – moving all that is not immediately necessary and eliminating spatial distractions. Receding into the wall, the kitchen is hidden from view when not needed. When retracted, the empty space allows a table to pivot around, creating a clean work area with an unobstructed view across the pool. Located in the centre of the room, the pool and suspended fireplace anchor the space as the only fixed elements. Separated by water from the work and kitchen space, the living area contains a bed that sinks into the floor, allowing a couch to fold out from the wall. A sanctuary where everything works in unison, Womb represents a harmony of transformation bathed in the nuances of luminosity. Enveloping the inhabitant in an environment designed for reflection and escape, as well as constructive contemplation, it is at once a base for work, office and meditation.

TNT Woman

TNT Woman, Toronto, 2001

Located in Toronto's Yorkville district – once a derelict collection of hippie flop-houses – the *parti* of TNT Woman revolves around two critical design elements: frame-like partitions of powder-coated steel and a circular, cash-counter clad in stainless steel. TNT Woman is the flagship of a series of stores including Man, Intimates and Blu. While each store has its own identity, they are aesthetically part of the same family. Highlighted with glass and accented with light – including a single red gelled fluorescent – TNT Woman's three translucent wardrobes house the majority of the merchandise within single clean forms. While the clothes are openly displayed on stainless-steel rails and cantilevered pivoting shelves, window-shoppers see only ghosted silhouettes, adding to the store's theatrical and erotic milieu. Dramatically centred within the triangular space, the single-cylindrical form of the cash desk references the feminine and seduces passers-by with its sensual and voluminous curves. Acting as a transition between these spaces, an unexpected suspended glass lantern illuminates the freestanding mannequin stands. While the store's minimalist aesthetic is highly logical, it is also interestingly paradoxical. Chou sees his space as a refuge from the harsh realities of the outside world, yet he intentionally blurs the distinction between the two. Nevertheless, he ritualises the experience of shopping by celebrating and amplifying this process of transition. ⋑

Below
As seen here on a tree in the Narivara freshwater swamp in Trinidad, in marshy ground the roots
of a tree are able to support the structure above by spreading the load and gripping the mud.
Allowances can be made for movements in the ground with additional root growth. Foundations
for man-made buildings are very difficult to design in these unstable ground conditions.

Building with Genes

This article by **Bill Watts** poses a window into a new way of working and thinking. What happens if, instead of looking at nature as simply a source of natural materials for the built environment, you start regarding it as a catalogue of highly evolved systems from which to draw and learn?

Biological systems have evolved over the past three billion years to provide a rich array of mechanisms and constructs that are utilised in living organisms today, ourselves included. The living world can provide all the products we need to build and service our built environment. This is clear from more primitive times when we lived in shelters made with wood, leather and straw, and used wood or dung for heat and light. How this could be done now without a major change to our current Western style of living needs some explanation.

As we have learnt to manipulate the earth's mineral resources and use the fossilised energy from plants laid down over millions of years, our standard of living has improved. The logical conclusion that drawing from stored resources, using them once and discarding the waste in a linear fashion is unsustainable, is only just starting to dawn on us.

But there is another route. I will be exploring here how the systems of the living world might be used to create a built environment where all the materials used are recycled, and the only energy input is the sun. This is a fundamental aspect of all stable ecosystems. Within some limited constraints there are biological analogues to our current methods of construction to maintain our current quality of life without having to go back to burning dung.

The possibilities for these systems are enormous.

The structural properties of wood are well understood and used. However, we are not exploiting the full potential of the strength of the material to build structures as high as the giant redwood trees that reach heights of 100 metres with extensive canopies cantilevered away from the central trunk. We need stable and predictable inorganic materials such as steel and concrete to build this high. Dead wood will twist and shrink, causing chaos in a tall static structure. On the other hand, living wood can grow to compensate for structural problems using the same gravity-sensing control mechanisms that make stems grow straight up. Particular areas of structural concern on a windy site can be thickened and strengthened with appropriate growth.

Redwoods are several thousand years old. The biomass in them was created using the solar energy falling on the leaves of the tree over its life. Being impatient we would want to speed up this process by using larger areas of land to gather the solar energy and create the biomass more quickly. I estimate the weight of a two-storey 100-square-metre wooden house to be 30 tonnes. With biomass production at 12 oven-dried tonnes per hectare per year (willow coppice in good ground in the UK), it would take two and a half years to grow the 30 tonnes in a hectare. The material would then need to be assembled on site.

If the structure were grown in flat panels, the ability of organisms to grow and heal could be used to fix the elements together and assemble the building.

Man-made substructures rely largely on the mass of concrete footings and the friction on the side of piles to the surrounding ground. Trees are supported by an extensive branched matrix of roots that grip the soil far more effectively and with less material than man-made foundations. Traditionally, foundations are designed with much margin to deal with settlement in the ground. A dynamic living system can deal with these changes to the ground conditions better than a static one, by compensatory growth.

Top left
Electron micrograph of a muscle fibre: the pink and yellow bands are the contractile elements that generate movement; the brown blobs are the mitochondria that produce the ATP molecules used to drive the movement mechanisms.

Bottom left
The cycle of high-energy ATP and low-energy ADP molecules that drive the energy-using functions in all life systems.

Below
As a biological source of light, these fireflies help illuminate the cave.

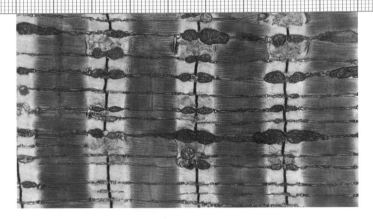

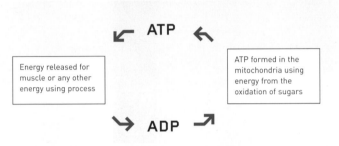

ATP

Energy released for muscle or any other energy using process

ATP formed in the mitochondria using energy from the oxidation of sugars

ADP

Using living systems introduces other possibilities of meeting our servicing needs that require energy flows. Movement, heat, light and even electricity are generated in the living world. Heart muscle can generate three to five watts of power/kilogram without fatigue. A skeletal muscle can produce up to 100 watts/kilogram but only for short periods. This compares with electric motors which can produce in the range of 15 watts of power per kilogram for small (10- to 100-watt) motors rising to 100+ watts/kilogram for larger ones. Bioluminescence is used in a number of species from fireflies to dinoflagellates. Electrical impulses are used throughout the animal kingdom in the nervous control systems, but high-voltage generation has evolved in only a limited number of animals for predatory uses. Heat is a by-product of generating any of these energy products from chemical energy in much the same way as it is in a power station.

The energy for all of these processes comes from the same molecular currency of oxidising adenosine triphosphate (ATP) high-energy molecules to adenosine diphosphate (ADP). ATP is in turn created from ADP, using the energy released from oxidising sugars. This all occurs in mitochondria, organelles that are present in all cells. This system evolved very early in the history of life, and the flux of ATP/ADP between the mitochondria and the energy-consuming processes in a cell is a common and constant component throughout the living world. The raw energy sources can be many and various, but all come from the product of photosynthesis at the bottom of the food chain.

A building can to a certain extent feed itself from the solar energy falling on the roof, walls and surrounding garden, but more may be required. This could be supplemented from imported foodstuffs which could be fed to the building.

One can see how a room could be ventilated, heated and lit with these low-energy densities.

If bioluminescence can operate at the same energy density as heart muscle, the ceiling of a room would need to be lined with one to two millimetres of luminant cells to produce enough light for office standards. If the cells were separated out into red, yellow and blue light phosphors, the colour of the light could be altered or images displayed as on an LCD flat screen. To do this one would need to control each cell, or 'pixel', individually at a high rate. This technology already exists, albeit in reverse, in visual systems where a huge amount of information is gathered in the rod and cone cells in the eye and processed in real time in the brain.

Heating, ventilation and cooling are all processes that are necessary in the living world and could be adapted to buildings. Ventilation can be through an outside wall. There are many systems that control the porosity of an outer layer of an organism to gas exchange, such as stomata in leaves. As the air passes through the walls it can be filtered, heated and treated in other ways, for example the addition of (pleasant) smells. The gas exchange could be via straight diffusion, as is the case within a leaf, aided by other natural ventilation forces that we use in buildings (wind and stack pressures). Alternatively, ventilation can be powered by the flexing of one of the surfaces in the room acting as a large diaphragm. A one-millimetre displacement of a square metre of ceiling has a volume

Left
A section through the retina of the eye. The rods and cones, stained in grey, are distinguished by their shapes. The field of view is 0.075 millimetres across. If these cells were producing light rather than sensing it, the definition of the image would be better than a VDU.

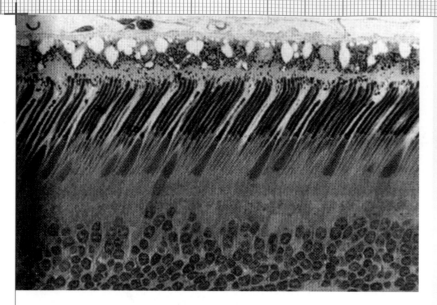

of one litre. If it were to cycle once a second it would provide the one litre/second per square metre of fresh air that the room needs. Greater deflections will generate larger volumes and pressures. The power and energy required for these systems is distributed and within the capabilities of a biological system. The power required by an electrically powered ventilation system is about one watt/litre per second. At three watts/kilogram this would require only a third of a kilogram of muscle/square metre of ceiling, or a sheet less than one millimetre thick. Other mechanisms could include peristalsis, as used in moving food around in the digestive system, or beating cilia.

The advantage of using powered ventilation is that one has control over the movement of the air and can put it through various systems to recover heat or moisture while allowing the air to pass. With a reciprocating system, the air can be passed through a matrix of material that can absorb heat and moisture from the air going in one direction and return it to the air coming back in the opposite direction. This is found in the camel's nose to save moisture loss from its lungs, and in man-made reciprocating heat exchangers. In a heating mode the recovery will reduce the amount of energy required for heat. Indeed, the efficiency of the heat exchange and the resistance to the airflow can increase as it gets colder outside. The muscular effort and the heat produced will go up as the resistance, which could be tailored to meet the heating needs of the space, increases. Evaporative cooling can also be added to the system.

Deep-plan buildings cannot rely on the air coming through the walls, so a powered ventilation system could be used in much the same way as the man-made equivalent. However, there is the opportunity to do all the servicing of an internal room using a liquid circulation system to provide cooling and oxygen, and to take away carbon dioxide and pollutants to central plant areas containing gas exchange and waste removal systems (lungs, kidneys etc). The human waste would be welcomed by the building as a useful source of

nutrients. A well-integrated building system like this would need the circulatory systems that are found in higher plants and animals to transport the chemical energy and waste products around the building. It would also need a nervous system to control the various processes that take place within the building. There are life forms of the scale of buildings so one should not doubt that systems on this scale are possible.

We have been harnessing the products of the living world to the best of our ability by selectively breeding organisms to develop traits that we find useful or interesting. This has produced high-yield wheat varieties and bulldogs. However, the organisms still require significant management and processing to make them useful to us. Plywood comes from trees that have been shaved into thin sheets and glued together – it would be more convenient if it grew in flat panels in the first place.

Our level of understanding of how life systems work, grow and are controlled is becoming more and more sophisticated. We also have the ability to patch together the genes that form the blueprint of life. The power of the research tools and number of people in the field means that our knowledge is expanding rapidly. Society's imperative is to find answers to human medical problems, and the fact that this work is producing good exciting pure science is driving this research. Apart from breakthroughs such as the complete sequencing of the human genome, work is quietly going on in labs around the world on myriad subjects away from the public's gaze. The pure and applied aspects of this science are contributing to building an increasingly refined picture of living systems.

I believe that it is only a matter of time before the immense complexities of the living world are understood well enough to enable us to re-create, at will, living objects that we have designed to suit our needs. The opportunities to displace current man-made processes and manufactured goods with living organisms designed by humans from scratch is immense. And the temptation to use this knowledge to harness the living world in a cheap and sustainable manner will be as irresistible as fire, flight or nuclear power. △

In the forthcoming issues of △, André Chaszar, an engineer who is on sabbatical from Buro Happold while pursuing research in CAD/CAM as well as teaching and consulting independently in New York, will explore the current uses and especially the potential of CAD/CAM for architecture, engineering and construction.

Bill Watts did a degree in zoology at Oxford followed by two years studying fish behaviour in Scotland. In 1980 he joined Max Fordham Consulting Engineers to design building services in a holistic manner. Through his work on various building types he has developed an understanding of how buildings are put together, the energy flows through them and how to make them function elegantly, drawing parallels with the physiology of organisms in the living world.

Below top
Plasticity: 'Rather sensuous, more like a female body in contrast to
sharp-angled male architecture.' — F Kiesler

Below bottom
'Josef Kaplicky was my father. I owe him quite a lot. He gently introduced
me to architecture, culture, art, everything. He was a sculptor, painter,
graphic designer, writer and architect himself.' — Jan Kaplicky

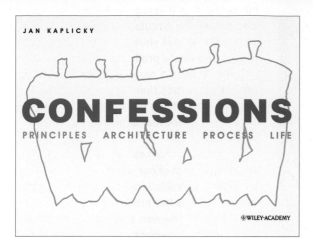

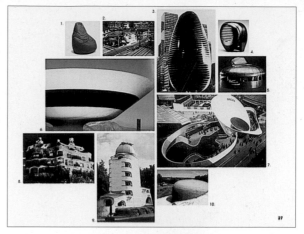

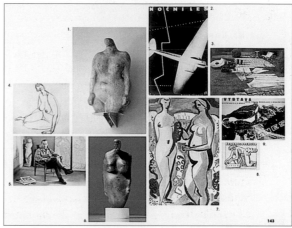

CONFESSIONS:
PRINCIPLES ARCHITECTURE PROCESS LIFE

*What is there to confess? All? Something? Nothing? It is all
about what you feel inside, as an architect, as an individual,
as a man? How to express your feelings within your work?
How to resist so many wrong temptations? Commercial
pressures. Financial needs. Comforts. Glory. Poverty. Survival.
Attacks. Jealousy. Arrogance. Very rarely praises. How to
survive horrible people, bad television, bad books, ugly people?
How to be strong enough every single morning, organise your
mind, and above all create something?* — Jan Kaplicky

Jan Kaplicky, founder of London firm Future Systems, is an
unorthodox architect, and *Confessions* is an unorthodox
autobiography. As Kaplicky says: 'Architecture is my life, not
just my profession'. This, therefore, is a book about an
architectural life, private and professional. It offers an insight
into the mind of this fascinating architect – his experiences,
ideas, opinions and sources of inspiration.

Confessions is a highly personal account that avoids the
speculations and intellectualisations of critical theory. It is a
collection of comments on architects, architecture, design,
politics, beauty, people and the future.

The book is divided into four sections: 'Principles',
'Architecture', 'Process' and 'Life'. Each has an equal
balance of images and textual observations, so that it is
both visually and mentally engaging, and its spontaneous,
honest style makes it accessible to a wide audience.
The first section sets out the essential elements behind all
creative acts, emphasising the need for freedom in order
for creativity to flourish, and giving pointers to the most
vital factors in good design – poetry, elegance, sensuality,
plasticity, colour and the 'magic final touch' of sexuality.
The second addresses the state of the architectural
profession today and speculates on possible future
developments. The third examines the creative process,
from form-finding using a diverse range of influences

to the pros and cons of teamwork, and describes the
development of Future Systems. Finally, the fourth
section catalogues Kaplicky's memories from early
childhood to today, including his wartime experiences
in Prague, his relationship with his parents which
nurtured his creative instincts, his flight to the West,
and the development of his professional and private
life since his arrival in London in 1968, as he worked
his way through several major architectural practices
before founding his own firm.

Kaplicky stresses the importance of maintaining a
free and open mind in order to effect positive progress
in architecture. He calls for greater consideration
of people and the environment in architectural design,
and looks to every aspect of life for inspiration.
His refreshing approach to architecture and to life itself
is bound to provide stimulus for anyone who picks
up this book, whether professionals in the field or
general readers with an interest in creative culture
– architectural, visual or otherwise. ⌂

CONFESSIONS: PRINCIPLES, ARCHITECTURE, PROCESS, LIFE
was published by Wiley-Academy (London) in July 2002.
It is available from bookshops or from
www.wileyeurope.com at £24.95.

Below
Allford, Hall, Monaghan and Morris, exterior of Monsoon HQ, 2002.

Monsoon HQ

David Hamilton Eddy looks at how Allford, Hall, Monaghan and Morris were able to retain the 'simplicity and honesty' of the original Paddington Maintenance Depot in their conversion of a London landmark for the fashion retailer Monsoon.

When driving back to London one's return to Marylebone Road is signalled by a smoothly curvaceous building. It has always been rather mysterious, seemingly floating by the edge of Westway; nothing identified it except its shape.

It is a truly streamlined building apparently drifting past my illusorily stationary car; that was how Erich Mendelsohn had described the relationship between road traffic and his own 'floating' streamlined buildings in Germany in the 1920s. A building that unpeels as you drive by, an authentic Futurist building that is predicated on speed – architecture that is symbiotic with the motor car, virtuous architecture redolent of strength, power and energy.

The architect Simon Allford experienced this building as 'magical' long before his partnership of Allford, Hall, Monaghan and Morris (AHMM) was given the brief to convert it into offices for the fashion chain Monsoon Ltd.

But to convert it from what? Winner of an △D Project Award in 1966 (△D, April 1966), the Paddington Maintenance Depot with its accompanying rotunda sister building, both listed Grade II* in 1994, was designed in 1964 by architects Bicknell and Hamilton to provide new maintenance workshops for 'vehicles and plant and warehousing, displaced due to the extension of Western Avenue' (△D, January 1969).

The flowing form of the building was 'conditioned by the form of the new road works, already designed' (△D, January 1969). Paul Hamilton, the partner in charge of the original project, explained that he was used to working with British Rail, having designed signal boxes and other structures for the

company, and that 'the original design decision was a consequence of the strictures of the site and the requirements of the brief for British Rail'. Moreover, 'the rounded shapes of the depot [now Monsoon HQ] and adjoining rotunda were conditioned by the practical demands of large wheeled trucks with their specific turning circles'. Vehicles move in curves. 'The design developed as a natural progression according to the particular needs of the brief'. It was only after the building was completed that Hamilton recognised the resemblance to Mendelsohn's Universum Cinema in Berlin with its 'film strip' fenestration similar to that of the Paddington building.

Hamilton's implicit point that the process of design has its own integrity is an important one, interestingly later independently confirmed by Simon Allford. In answer to my question, Allford asserted that it wasn't a question of curved versus rectilinear. Even in a completely curved building there are right-angles in the interior grid. Speaking specifically of the Paddington building he stated: 'Of course, the building is streamlined. It reminded me of Cedric Price's Lyons Corner House in Blackpool. Streamlining is part of the repertoire and reservoir of architecture. It's not necessary to have camps and battles. The manifestoes of the early part of the last century were a means, a tool for design'.

Allford wanted to reflect the simplicity and honesty of the building in AHMM's conversion. For example,

Below
Allford, Hall, Monaghan and Morris, interior of Monsoon HQ, 2002.

Below top
Paul A Hamilton, model of Paddington Maintenance Depot, 1966.

Below bottom
Erich Mendelsohn, Woga Complex (incl. Universum Cinema), Berlin, 1926–28.

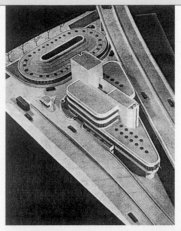

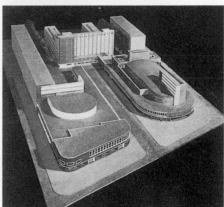

there would be no suspended ceilings. What AHMM wanted was: 'You wouldn't know we'd been there'. The original long-life, loose-fit approach was continued in the conversion. Any suitable media company could fit into the building.

Still, changes had to be made. Access to the building in its role as Monsoon HQ was a problem. A new 50-metre route involving a ramp and pedestrian bridge across the Grand Union Canal at Little Venice, as an integrated part of the general office development of the Paddington Basin, inspired a large three-storey atrium entrance, cut out of the existing structure, that provided direct access both to the newly converted double lifts (replacing the old 10-tonne capacity industrial lift) and, on the other side, to Hamilton's superb stairwell with its original Japanese ceramic tiles. In the middle was a suitably informal reception area.

Allford remarked on the fine quality of the structure of the building after years of disuse when the interior had provided the backdrop for countless illegal raves as well as lending its walls to some of the most artistic graffiti in London.

The sheer strength of the building was due to the fact that Maunsell & Partners, the original structural engineers, had used traditional high-grade concrete. Not for nothing had Maunsell given its name to the concrete channel forts of the First World War. This in turn reminds us that Mendelsohn had been inspired by the curved lines of First World War military concrete bunkers for the streamlined form of the Einstein Tower; curved concrete helped deflect the penetrating power of projectiles.

The Monsoon building has to be one of the best office buildings in London. Particularly noteworthy is the spacious café overlooking the approaching traffic returning to London on Westway. The sense of relaxation inherent here is reprised throughout the office spaces, the uterine quality of which facilitates an easy circulation on every floor. There is a nice balance between the slightly untidy, evidently working work stations and the overall smooth, clean sense of horizontality in the fenestration curving round the large spaces. Here, too, the exterior curve of the stairwell is at one with the curve of the office walls – a soothing concentricity.

It is rare these days to experience architecture so directly pleasurable and calming. It is a relief from the orthodoxies of hi-tech, itsy-bitsy deconstruction, flamboyant, more or less ironic Postmodernism or the 'normal' corporate glassy cube. Experiencing the Monsoon we remember that architecture can be great like Frank Lloyd Wright's Guggenheim Museum is great – great in that special idiosyncratic way as demonstrated by the Modern Movement. Such memories are the only guide we have to what is truly virtuous in architectural design. ∆

David Hamilton Eddy has written about architecture for 30 years drawing on his interests in literature and psychology to develop his own brand of architectural criticism. He has a particular interest in Erich Mendelsohn. Otherwise he hangs out with his fictional alter ego, the Atlanta private investigator Eddie Jackson.

Subscribe Now for 2003

As an influential and prestigious architectural publication, *Architectural Design* has an almost unrivalled reputation worldwide. Published bimonthly, it successfully combines the currency and topicality of a newsstand journal with the editorial rigour and design qualities of a book. Consistently at the forefront of cultural thought and design since the 1960s, it has time and again proved provocative and inspirational – inspiring theoretical, creative and technological advances. Prominent in the 1980s for the part it played in Postmodernism and then in Deconstruction, Δ has recently taken a pioneering role in the technological revolution of the 1990s. With groundbreaking titles dealing with cyberspace and hypersurface architecture, it has pursued the conceptual and critical implications of high-end computer software and virtual realities. Δ

Δ Architectural Design

SUBSCRIPTION RATES 2003
Institutional Rate: UK £160
Personal Rate: UK £99
Discount Student* Rate: UK £70
OUTSIDE UK
Institutional Rate: US $240
Personal Rate: US $150
Student* Rate: US $105

*Proof of studentship will be required when placing an order. Prices reflect rates for a 2002 subscription and are subject to change without notice.

TO SUBSCRIBE
Phone your credit card order:
+44 (0)1243 843 828

Fax your credit card order to:
+44 (0)1243 770 432

Email your credit card order to:
cs-journals@wiley.co.uk

Post your credit card or cheque order to:
John Wiley & Sons Ltd.
Journals Administration Department
1 Oldlands Way
Bognor Regis
West Sussex PO22 9SA
UK

Please include your postal delivery address with your order.

All Δ volumes are available individually. To place an order please write to:
John Wiley & Sons Ltd
Customer Services
1 Oldlands Way
Bognor Regis
West Sussex PO22 9SA

Please quote the ISBN number of the issue(s) you are ordering.

Δ is available to purchase on both a subscription basis and as individual volumes

---

○ I wish to subscribe to Δ *Architectural Design* at the **Institutional rate of £160.**

○ I wish to subscribe to Δ *Architectural Design* at the **Personal rate of £99.**

○ I wish to subscribe to Δ *Architectural Design* at the **Student rate of £70.**

STARTING FROM ISSUE 1/2003.

○ Payment enclosed by Cheque/Money order/Drafts.

Value/Currency £/US$ [   ]

○ Please charge £/US$ [   ] to my credit card.
Account number:

[ ][ ][ ][ ][ ][ ][ ][ ][ ][ ][ ][ ][ ][ ][ ][ ]

Expiry date:

[ ][ ][ ][ ][ ][ ]

Card: Visa/Amex/Mastercard/Eurocard *(delete as applicable)*

Cardholder's signature [   ]

Cardholder's name [   ]

Address [   ]

[   ]

Post/Zip Code [   ]

Recipient's name [   ]

Address [   ]

[   ]

Post/Zip Code [   ]

I would like to buy the following Back Issues at £22.50 each:

○ Δ 159 *Versioning in Architecture*, SHoP

○ Δ 158 *Furniture + Architecture*, Edwin Heathcote

○ Δ 157 *Reflexive Architecture*, Neil Spiller

○ Δ 156 *Poetics in Architecture*, Leon van Schaik

○ Δ 155 *Contemporary Techniques in Architecture*, Ali Rahim

○ Δ 154 *Fame and Architecture*, J. Chance and T. Schmiedeknecht

○ Δ 153 *Looking Back in Envy*, Jan Kaplicky

○ Δ 152 *Green Architecture*, Brian Edwards

○ Δ 151 *New Babylonians*, Iain Borden + Sandy McCreery

○ Δ 150 *Architecture + Animation*, Bob Fear

○ Δ 149 *Young Blood*, Neil Spiller

○ Δ 148 *Fashion and Architecture*, Martin Pawley

○ Δ 147 *The Tragic in Architecture*, Richard Patterson

○ Δ 146 *The Transformable House*, Jonathan Bell and Sally Godwin

○ Δ 145 *Contemporary Processes in Architecture*, Ali Rahim

○ Δ 144 *Space Architecture*, Dr Rachel Armstrong

○ Δ 143 *Architecture and Film II*, Bob Fear

○ Δ 142 *Millennium Architecture*, Maggie Toy and Charles Jencks

○ Δ 141 *Hypersurface Architecture II*, Stephen Perrella

○ Δ 140 *Architecture of the Borderlands*, Teddy Cruz

○ Δ 139 *Minimal Architecture II*, Maggie Toy

○ Δ 138 *Sci-Fi Architecture*, Maggie Toy

○ Δ 137 *Des-Res Architecture*, Maggie Toy